1984

LUVO ● MAQUELA DO ZOMBO
ÃO SALVADOR ●
MADIMBA ● ● MAVOIO

● M'BRIDGE

SONGO●

● CARMONA
NEGAGE ●
● QUITEXE

● LOANDA ● MALANGE

A N G O L A

The Fabric of Terror

BERNARDO TEIXEIRA

The Fabric of

Terror

Three Days in Angola

Introduction by Robert Ruark

Afterword by James Burnham

Illustrations by Julio Gil

The Devin-Adair Company
New York   1965

Canadian Agent: Abelard-Schuman Canada, Ltd., Toronto
Library of Congress Catalog Card Number 65-13914
Manufactured in the United States of America

Designed by Ernest Reichl

Contents

Introduction by Robert Ruark		vii
Author's Foreword		xi
1	Return of the Weeds	1
2	The Fabric of Terror	15
3	The Massacre at Quitexe	33
4	The Battle of Carmona	43
5	The Sawmill at Luvo	75
6	The Leader	91
7	Tranquility at Mavoio	103
8	A Prayer for Madimba	113
9	The Photographs	123
10	The Execution	139
11	The Avenger	147
Afterword by James Burnham		157
Photographs: The Proof		
Between pages 80 and 81		

Introduction

BY ROBERT RUARK

The author of this book comes from an old Portuguese family, and he knows the jungles of Georgetown in Washington, D.C. and the halls of the United Nations in New York and the horse country of Virginia as well as he knows Lisbon and Estoril in his homeland.

But Bernardo ("Tony") Teixeira knows other things as well. He knows the backbush of Portuguese Angola, and he is no stranger to Mozambique. I know he is no stranger to those countries because I was out there with him.

I am no stranger to violence in Africa, either, since I was in Kenya from the start of the Mau Mau almost until the time that the Mau Mau wound up in the cabinet of the freshly *Uhuru*-ed Kenya. In point of fact I became expert on violence, if you will admit two books of mine, *Something of Value* and *Uhuru* into evidence.

But nothing that I wrote fictionally can compare to the stark, horrid facts of Tony Teixeira's book, *Fabric of Terror*.

What has been happening in Angola is a nightmare, a terrible perversion of the rights of man, black and white. The crime has been committed cynically by hired strangers—strangers drunk on the local *pombe*, strangers fired by hashish, strangers recruited and semitrained across the northern Angolese border in the Congo, strangers with no real ax to grind except against an innocent neck, strangers who have been armed by the terrorists of Algeria, strangers motivated by Russia and China and other Communist affiliates.

The rapes and tortures and robberies and obscenities and arsons committed by these strangers were, in one day, March 15, 1961, worse than the combined atrocities of the Portuguese in 500 years of colonization—worse than the Germans in Tanganyika, worse than the Belgians in the central Congo. I have seen the pictures of just one day of horror, and they do not bear description, even if you have a broad knowledge of Mau Mau.

March 15 was planned and expertly executed over a 500-mile front, and the execution was carried out by a collection of Bakongos from the central Congo and northern Angola. The troops did not hunger and thirst for freedom; they hungered for rape and thirsted for blood.

God knows the Portuguese were toughly dominant in

their occupancy of the African territories they colonized. Perhaps they were not so cynical as the Americans, in their treatment of the Indians, or so stupidly arrogant as the British in their administration of the Raj. At least the Portuguese bedded with the natives and married with the natives, and never really discriminated racially against the natives.

I have been four times to Mozambique in the last two years, and I have walked, driven, or flown over the entire country. I know Angola from one end to the other. The most unhappy people in both countries are not the true natives. They are the white newcomers from Portugal who are either settlers, servants, clerks or soldiers.

Certainly in Mozambique the educational, health and other facilities in the towns and cities are superior to what so unproudly we hail in America. There is no problem of "integration" in Portuguese Africa. Interracially, it has always been integrated, and the lowliest bush native is a prince compared to a typical example of Harlem's ghettos.

The tragedy of the last outposts of what is called "colonialism" by the same people who gutted Hungary and Poland and the rest of the satellite states is that the so-called "freedom" movements are directed from outposts in Russia, China, Algeria, Tanganyika and the Congo. None of these states can manage its own business. The "freedom-fighters" never lived in the countries they are "freeing."

This "freedom" so far has amounted to horrid massacres

and razed farms. The weeds have reclaimed the efforts that people like Vasco da Gama started. The innocent have been slaughtered, and certainly the terrorists have killed more of their own color than of the allegedly hated *Wazungu*, the white man.

I will not detract from the book's impact by describing its contents. But if you can read "The Execution," the "Return of the Weeds," and "The Fabric of Terror" chapters in Tony Teixeira's book without questioning what goes on in this determined effort to wreck what is really the most basically sound relationship between white and black in Africa, I shall be very much surprised.

Teixeira is not writing bias nor is he writing justification of past sins. He is writing of today's cops and robbers, today's gangsters and good guys, today's cowboys in white hats and cowboys in black hats.

He is writing the truth. And in these days truth seems a hard commodity to sell. I believe Tony has managed to sell the truth.

Author's Foreword

THIS is not a book of fiction. It is a dramatized account of several true episodes, out of many, of the terrorist war in northern Angola—each one of them being a part of the record of recent human memory. This book does not attempt to study motivations or to ascribe responsibilities. It is concerned, primarily, with the palpable nature of the tragedy which befell so many innocent victims on the fateful morning of March 15, 1961, and, with somewhat less brutality, for some weeks afterwards.

All the places described in this book are located in the Uige District of northern Angola, with the exception of Camabatela, Quitexe and the Fazenda by the Lué River which are situated a few kilometers south of the Uige border. Luvo, São Salvador, Madimba, Mavoio and Maquela do Zombo form a kind of semicircle, the extremities of which touch the Congo border. M'Bridge, Songo, Carmona and Negage are on a diagonal westeast, further south.

Chronologically, terror struck at about the same time in Luvo, the Primavera plantation (São Salvador) and M'Bridge, that is, in the very early hours of the morning of March 15. At Quitexe and the Fazenda by the Lué River, it happened nearly two hours later, at eight o'clock of that morning. At Mavoio, judging from a broken alarm clock, it must have been just before seven o'clock of the same morning. At Carmona, the terrorist assault did not start until the evening of the same day. At Madimba, it came the following day, March 16. In each assault the bands of terrorists were different ones, of course, with the possibility, however, that many of the terrorists who took part in the massacre at Primavera also participated at Madimba. And perhaps many of the killers at Quitexe, Songo and Nova Caipemba joined the evening assault on Carmona. But all the assaults appear to have been carefully synchronized by the U.P.A. organization in Leopoldville. The episodes related in the stories "The Execution," and "The Avenger" appear to have been "free lance" terrorist operations. The latter massacre at the Maria José Plantation (Negage), a strictly "black massacre," was locally directed but had responded to the call from the U.P.A. headquarters in Leopoldville. The U.P.A.—*União das Populações de Angola*—led by Holden Roberto, a friend and disciple of the late Patrice Lumumba, is the terrorist organization which claimed credit for the massacres in northern Angola.

Few times in the modern history of man have so many horrors and indignities been perpetrated upon the human being. Revisiting the places where the stains of blood were still fresh and listening intently to the recollections of those who lived through the nightmare brought me a sense of helplessness, as though all one could do now was to cry for the victims and feel shame and pity for the senseless killers. But, in the texture of aroused human emotions, murder and revenge are inseparable twins, and the chain cannot be stopped by merely turning one's head away from the horror. Yet millions, lulled by the UN, did turn their heads away. Have they again been awakened by the dead lying at the feet of Lumumba's statue in Stanleyville? They may turn away again, but the fabric of terror will be with them elsewhere.

To many of us, who still believe that the spiritual values of our civilization are a worthy heritage for our children, the gift of a pedantic or callous interpretation of the wheels of history and of the winds of political change is a poor gift indeed to cherish. Other values much closer to God are still permanent in our souls, and one of these values is the dignity of the human being. Without it, we shall revert to the law of the jungle, and tomorrow's sunrise may become again the morning of endless night.

B. T.

Washington, D.C.

The Fabric of Terror

1

Return of the Weeds

When I first visited the Fazenda by the Lué River more than a decade ago, it was a vast, beautiful and prosperous plantation growing some of the best coffee in Angola. Owned by my cousin, it was a little, happy world in itself, it seemed to me.

After working hours and all day Sunday, there was always a great deal of singing and dancing and flirtation among the young people. But it all changed abruptly on the misty morning of March 15, 1961—and this is the reason why, about a year later, I felt the sad desire to revisit the Fazenda by the Lué River. In that pilgrimage I was accompanied by an old friend who had also been the doctor for the family at the Fazenda.

We started out from Carmona, the capital of northern Angola, but when we arrived at the village of Quitexe, which was surrounded by hills sheltering several bands of guerrillas, we were given a military escort for the last leg of the trip.

THE doctor and I left Quitexe in a caravan going south toward the Dange heights along the Catixo road. The Dange heights were for the most part in the hands of terrorists, and the entire road south from Carmona to Caxito, through Quitexe, was still closed to civilian traffic. Our Land Rover was escorted by two jeeps and a semiarmored car carrying a detachment of *Caçadores Especiais* (Special Hunters), or commandos, from the company stationed at Quitexe. The officer in charge of the detachment was a young lieutenant who had been a law student in civilian life. He traveled in the Land Rover with us, an M-30 rifle resting on his knees and a small sack of hand grenades in a sling.

Outside Quitexe the terrain suddenly became steep

and the hills farther ahead on the right looked hostile and watchful.

"I have gone as far as the second of those brown hills yonder," the lieutenant said as he pointed ahead. "Beyond that point it is nearly impassable and suicidal."

We went on a few more kilometers before the jeep in the lead made a sharp turn to the left into a very narrow dirt road leading downhill to a small green valley by the Lué River. At a turn of the path the Fazenda appeared before our eyes in a kind of tranquil splendor and decay.

It was a lovely site, but on the rolling fertile ground the coffee was no longer growing. The wild weeds were mushrooming so rapidly and vigorously that, from a distance, they assumed the personality of trees. The fields and the pastures on the banks of the zigzagging river had been smothered by the frantically growing elephant grass, and the branches of the tropical jungle were stretching their arms across the narrow bed of the river to join the tall grass. Yet, there was a feeling of tranquil melancholy about this return of the land to the wild weeds and jungle trees, though the dark hills of Dange cast a somber shadow over the valley.

On a natural terrace in the center of the plantation, the house stood with an air of sovereignty despite the scars it bore and its rapid decay. It had been a large, white and modern home, its horseshoe wings spreading to the east and west, with blue tiles adorning the façade. In front and on both sides of the house, the artistically designed garden could only be imagined under the wild weeds, the advance guard of the conquering jungle. Below the terrace, on the slanted ground leading down to the river, were the skeletons of several smaller houses and barns, with mutilated walls and broken roofs, doors and windows; these must have been the houses of foremen and workers.

The tropical splendor of the main house was marred by deep scars; the fire had burned the roofs, windows and doors, leaving patches of black smokestain on the masonry and the tiles.

Our military column came to a stop in front of the silent burned mansion. The commandos jumped from their vehicles and deployed themselves in a circle around the terrace on which the house stood, but two soldiers remained in the armored car with the heavy machine gun.

We stood there in silence for a minute staring at the empty hollow which had been the main entrance to the house.

"Your cousin used to call the Fazenda his Versailles-sur Lué," the doctor remarked, to break the silence.

A mocking yellow bird beat its wings, with a great clatter, and then glided to the edge of the roof. It perched on the tip of a beam which had been turned into charcoal by the fire, and it seemed to be straining its tiny pupils to appraise the strange sight of the human beings below who stood motionless in their imitation leopard uniforms. Then, the bird began to sing or laugh, irritably.

"The graves are at the back of the house," the doctor said. "Your cousin's will specified that he and his family should be buried in the Fazenda."

We walked around the skeleton of the mansion and came to three lonely flat graves, protected by a low iron gate. A tall, mutilated wooden cross stood at the head of the graves. I became keenly aware of the silent backs of the soldiers watching the somber hills of Dange.

"Nobody really knows for certain what happened here, but it must have happened at about the same time the attack was made at Quitexe and many other places. Nobody got to the Fazenda until a week later," the doctor was saying. "For some weird reason the vultures spared the bodies. Perhaps the smoke from the smouldering fire of the houses, barns and crops kept the birds away. The only known survivor was an assistant foreman, a young white man who managed to grab a lead pipe as a weapon, kill a few of the attackers and evade his pursuers. Three dead terrorists were found here on this terrace with their skulls cracked, and the heavy pipe with blood stains on it was also found. But the young man has been more or less incoherent ever since and his stories get all mixed up. It is also probable that the young son had some warning and that he rushed to his father's room to grab an automatic to defend his mother. The mother, the son and a native housemaid were found in the lady's room with the bodies of two terrorists which had revolver bullets in them. Your cousin, the white foreman with his wife and three children, as well as the native butler and two other native housemaids were all found on the ground in front of the house, as though they had been caught by complete surprise. There was another fateful twist to this tragedy. Your younger cousin had arrived unexpectedly the day before from his prep school in Luanda to be with his mother for her birthday which would have been March 16 . . ."

The doctor was interrupted by the sound of four shots in the distance.

"Steady!" the lieutenant shouted at his soldiers. And he added, addressing us, "A handful of those clowns on the hill over there beyond the valley must have seen our vehicles. They are so thrilled with their new rifles donated by the Algerians that they could not contain themselves. They cannot reach us from there and they only exposed their presence. Sergeant!"

"Yes, sir," the sergeant said, coming to attention.

"On the way back, when we reach the entrance of the Fazenda, you will take half of our men on foot along that hilly slope to the left," the lieutenant instructed. "We will give you a fifteen minute advantage. Then we will start slowly toward the Caxito road where we will meet you. Half of your patrol should carry submachine guns and the other half rifles. Take a few hand grenades, for an emergency. Catch one fellow alive, if you can. Crawl as much as possible once you locate them. If you *do* locate them, try to push them toward the Caxito road. Use your walkie-talkie sparingly."

According to plan, when the column reached the gates of the Fazenda the sergeant and his detail dropped silently from their vehicles and crawled away through the elephant grass. The column continued its march very slowly, as the soldiers kept their eyes on the fringes of the tall grass and their fingers on the triggers.

"Was it very bad, doctor?" I asked.

"You mean the bodies at the Fazenda? . . . No worse than usual," the doctor answered vaguely, turning his head away. Then, on an impulse, he took a paper from his pocket and handed it to me.

"This is a copy of the transcript of the questioning of the assistant foreman," the doctor explained. "The young man had been found and brought to the Carmona hospital, suffering from shock. It is coherent in spots and incoherent in others."

"Where is he now?" I asked.

"To tell you the truth, I do not know," the doctor answered.

The transcript read:

"Q. Would you tell us in your own words what happened at the Fazenda?

"A. I and the foreman come up from our quarters at seven o'clock to meet with the boss in front of the house and we all sit down at the outdoor table under the *jinga* tree discussing the work plans for the day. The morning is very foggy. The *cassimbo* is so low that we can hardly see beyond the terrace. Two of the housemaids come out with coffee, rolls and sausage for us. The foreman's wife and her three children also come out from their quarters and the children begin to play American cowboys around the *jinga* tree. Past seven-thirty we finish our breakfast and talk, and there is no sign of the workers. 'The boys are certainly taking a long time for breakfast this morning,' the boss says. Then the Bakongo *capataz* and many of the workers begin to show up through the *cassimbo* on the terrace. The butler comes out with a pitcher of *aguardente* for them. They like it after breakfast. 'Where are the missing ones? And who are these new boys I have never seen before?' the foreman asks the Bakongo *capataz*. And the *capataz* says, 'Some of the Bailundos are sick in bed, boss, very sick, and I hired some of these volunteers yesterday.' The boss becomes suspicious and tells the butler, 'Run down to the workers' quarters and find out what happened to the missing Bailundos.' Then I see the foreman's wife give a little cry, as though something scares her, and she runs to her children still playing cowboys. Then I do not remember very well what happens except that I grab a piece of lead pipe, crack a couple of skulls of those jumping me, and manage to run away into the fog and hide in a hole in the bush. And I cover the hole with leaves. They are looking for me but they cannot find me.

"Q.   When the gang came up from the workers' quarters, did they have weapons in their hands?

"A.   Some of them carried their *catanas* which they use for cutting branches. Others had their heavy coats on, I think. I do not know if they are hiding weapons.

"Q.   Who was the person they attacked first?

"A.   The butler, I think, when he starts for the workers' quarters. But I am not sure.

"Q.   What was *happening* when you grabbed the piece of pipe to defend yourself?

"A.   I think some of them are setting fire to the house

and others are cutting up the boss, the foreman and the housemaids. It all happens very fast and there is a lot of screaming.

"Q. At that point, did you see the foreman's wife and her three children?

"A. I do not recall, sir. But I think I hear their screams.

"Q. Where was the Lady and the Master's son when this was happening on the terrace?

"A. They are in the house. Somebody locks the front door. The young master runs to his father's room, gets an automatic and goes into his mother's room. The *capataz* and the others are chopping at the door and they break it down and go after the Lady and her son.

"Q. How could you see all this happening inside the house when you had run out in the bush?

"A. I do not recall, sir.

"Q. Were you hiding *inside* the house when the terrorists broke in?

"A. Maybe, sir, but I do not recall. When I come to my senses I am hiding in a hole in the ground with leaves all over me.

"Q. Are you sure of that?

"A. I think so, sir. But I am not sure.

"Q. Were you very frightened when you were hiding inside the house and the terrorists were murdering the Lady and the young master?

"A. Yes, sir. But I do not recall hiding in the house.

"Q. But you saw the young master getting his father's revolver and going into his mother's room?

"A. I think I did, sir. But I am not sure.

"Q. How many days were you wandering around in the bush until you were found?

"A. Many days, I think, sir. But I am not sure."

I returned the paper to the doctor.

"Further questioning of the boy did not add anything to his original account," the doctor explained.

On the next bend of the narrow road, in a spot which appeared out of sight from the hill, the column came to a stop. With his forefinger to his nose the lieutenant indicated to us that he wanted absolute silence. He counted the time on his stop watch, as he kept his ear to the still silent walkie-talkie. Fifteen minutes later he gave a sign to the first jeep and the slow march was resumed. When we reached the Caxito road the column again came to a stop. No word had been heard yet from the sergeant.

"Let us meditate and smoke," the lieutenant whispered, as he offered us his package of cigarettes.

The minutes went by very slowly and chainsmoking went on very fast. But minutes later the dialogue of the birds in the wood to our left was rudely interrupted by the nervous staccato of submachine guns and rifle fire. The birds beat their wings madly and flew in disorder in all directions, but the rattling of the guns continued at the same frenzied rate for the next thirty seconds, then became sporadic, at last died away completely.

"All right, all right," the lieutenant was saying in the walkie-talkie. "I can hardly hear you . . . No, no, do not follow them. God knows where it will lead. Come back. We are at the intersection."

The lieutenant removed his helmet, pulled a handkerchief from his pocket and wiped his forehead.

"The patrol killed four of the clowns, but three others got away with the rifles of their dead. One of our boys was hurt," the lieutenant said, laconically.

Fifteen or twenty minutes later the commando detail returned, carrying a bleeding soldier on an improvised stretcher.

"Bring him here in the Land Rover. Lay him gently on the floor," the lieutenant instructed. "Doctor, would you take a look at this boy?"

The doctor was already leaning over the soldier, but when he lifted his head again his face was sad.

"This boy is dead," the doctor said.

The sergeant and his companions came quietly to attention. The officer paused for a few moments to take a close look at the dead soldier's face, and then he gently crossed the soldier's hands over his chest. He seemed to be searching for something to say.

"I will be missing this soldier. We get very used to each other's faces," the lieutenant said. "It is quite lonely up here."

2

The Fabric of Terror

The civilian pilot who took me from Luanda, capital of Angola, to Maquela do Zombo in the vicinity of the Congo border—the so-called "terrorist triangle"—was a pleasant and loquacious young man, born and raised in southern Angola among the Ganguela tribes whose virtues and whose skill at soccer he exalted. Although both his parents were European Portuguese, Vicente had never been out of Africa. His attitude towards the terrorist attacks of the previous year and the guerrilla warfare still going on was clinical rather than emotional. "It HAD to happen, and yet it COULD have been avoided," he told me once.

"MY FATHER used to say that there are more ways of dying than ways of living, and somehow one gets mentally conditioned to the variety of possibilities . . . in Africa, at least," said the pilot of the small monoplane which was taking me to Maquela do Zombo, a Portuguese outpost located less than twenty miles from the Congo border. "Yet, no one can get used to the idea of being sliced up in a grotesque fashion after death. That's why I think all these people who stayed in the northern region after the massacres and atrocities of last year are quite brave."

We were flying at low altitude over the warm greenery covering the rolling hills northeast of Luanda. The dry season had begun, the morning sun was bright and caressing, and the quiet countryside spreading under my eyes exuded a feeling of comfort.

"Down there . . ." the pilot called my attention to a small and peaceful-looking village by the dirt road, "that village is Ucua. On that fateful morning of March 15, Ucua, like many other places, was completely caught by surprise. Two settlers and their families managed to escape the terrorists and they tried to make their way towards Caxito, the small town I pointed out to you a while ago. They walked through the elephant grass, keeping the road as point of reference. But the women and the children became utterly exhausted, and they were left hiding in a spot by the creek, with two rifles and ammunition, and one of the two men on guard. The other man went on to Caxito for help."

The sleepy village of Ucua was rapidly disappearing from view, the monoplane began to climb sharply to fly over the crest of a hill ahead, and the pilot had to raise his voice to be heard above the roar of the engine.

"When the man finally returned with help from Caxito," he continued, "everybody had been slain and beheaded. The terrorists had also cut off the limbs of some, and left them dangling from the branches of trees nearby. By the way, this kind of horror was one of their favorite atrocities. The man who returned with help went out of his mind. He tried to kill every black person in sight. He had to be put in a strait jacket in the hospital at Luanda, but he managed to jump out of a hospital window and kill himself."

Presently the clear skies became cloudier and cloudier, and the pilot gained further altitude to avoid the *cassimbo* shrouding the heights of Dange.

"The *cassimbo* has a particular predilection for this region," he explained. "We may not be able to enjoy the view until we clear the Mucaba mountain."

Indeed, when we flew over Carmona, the capital of northern Angola, the town was completely invisible beneath a thick veil of mist.

"To your left, if you could see it, is the village of Songo," the pilot said, a few minutes later. "One of the most bizarre atrocities to my knowledge took place on a plantation somewhere down there. A former classmate of mine used to run the small coffee plantation. He lived there with an African girl, his mistress. It wasn't until four or five days after the fifteenth of March that a group of vigilantes and soldiers managed to make their way to the plantation. They did find the body of the girl, beheaded and raped, as usual. But they could find no trace of my classmate or of any part of his body."

I turned my head away to stare at the *cassimbo* which was caressing the tips of our wings with its misty grey fingers.

"Here, take one of these. It will settle your stomach," he said, extending to me an open box of white pills. "Well, a couple of weeks later somebody found my classmate, purely by accident. You know, in some of these isolated farm places they don't have deep freezers because they haven't got any electricity. So, they keep certain perishables, especially the pork meat, in a large salt box. You can guess what happened. The terrorists stole the pork and put my classmate, all cut up, in the salt box. Funny thing is, whenever foreign newspapermen show up here and you try to tell them some of these true happenings, they usually stare at you with disbelief and indignation, as though you haven't got the right to speak evil of these sadistic murderers. Of course, there is also the language barrier. Few of us speak enough English or French to describe these things clearly. We are by now so used to the tales of these horrors that we hardly bother to tell them to strangers."

"Down below under the thick cloud is the village of Mucaba," the pilot said, interrupting a long silence, "You *must* have heard of it. That is the village where a handful of people held on for hours and hours in the church against hundreds of terrorists, sending SOS messages by an amateur shortwave transmitter. A few planes came up from the Negage air base, but the clouds were like today, low and thick, and they had to turn back. All but one. The people in the church had just about exhausted their ammunition and begun their prayers when this one fighter plane took a long chance through a hole in the low clouds and came upon the scene just in time. The small village has only one street, with the church at the very end of it. The pilot made a couple of runs from the opposite end of the street to the church, dropping small napalm bombs as he passed. The flames from the explosions almost reached his wings, and he barely missed the church in one of his passes. At any rate, more than half of the surprised terrorists were burned to a crisp and the others fled to the Mucaba mountain where many of them still are. The Mucaba mountain is right below us now. What would happen if my engine went off and I had to crash land on some clearing below? I give you one guess."

The skies began to clear up again on the other side of Mucaba and within an hour we made our approach for the landing at the makeshift airstrip at Maquela do Zombo.

The desolate-looking little town had an air of fatalism about it, as though it fully expected to be unloved by the visitor on first sight—as though the only memorable thing it could offer was its long and impressive name. However, militarily speaking, it is but a stone's throw from the Congo border, close to the heart of terrorism land.

A young and tall officer, wearing the inevitable camouflage uniform and carrying a submachine gun under his arm and a bush knife in his belt, met us as we landed and examined our papers perfunctorily.

"Welcome to the Paris of northern Angola," he said, as he gave us a rather ironic military salute. "Unfortunately, the hotel accommodations are not too satisfactory, particularly because no hotel has been built yet, and the same goes for the nightclubs and the movie houses. The local feminine talent is mostly Bakongo and hidden somewhere beyond the trees. But there are plenty of willing snakes in the elephant grass, if you are a charmer."

I complimented him on his sense of humor.

"After one year in this rotten spot, I can assure you, my dear sir, that the balance between sanity and insanity rests precisely on what you so flatteringly called my sense of humor," the lieutenant said, bowing his head slightly.

Presently he guided me to the house of the civil administrator where I was to have dinner and stay overnight, while my pilot stayed in the officers' quarters at the military barracks.

The house, located a few yards away from the end of the runway, was a rather large but unimaginative two-story stone structure with a small terrace facing the side of the bush. That side of the property was protected by a strong barbed wire fence. Beyond the fence, toward the bush, the tall grass had been cut for about two hundred yards to afford some warning in case of terrorist attack. On the small garden in front of the house wild flowers and cabbage grew in separate beds. Two neatly uniformed African sentries stood by the barbed wire, keeping their eyes on the bush ahead.

"They are Ganguelas from southern Angola," the lieutenant explained, "They hate Bakongos even more than I do, if that is possible. But we use them for guard duty only."

The hostess was waiting for us at the door. She was a very attractive woman in her early thirties whom I had met before in Luanda. Her sensuous red lips and her glossy black hair blended harmoniously with the remoteness of the place, but her deliberately chic appearance, from the delicate Italian shoes and elegant cocktail dress to her meticulously manicured fingernails, seemed a little incongruous at Maquela do Zombo. And the look in her eyes was not the same as I remembered from our first meeting—it was as though she was attempting to overcome the constant expectancy of danger by concentrating on her physical appearance. I noticed that the handsome lieutenant had taken longer than necessary to kiss her hand.

"It is so wonderful to see an old friend again," she said, addressing me. And she added, with a melancholy smile, "It was most gracious of you to come all the way from America to dine with us. Let me show you to your room. Then, we shall have a cocktail."

The living room, where I presently joined her for a cocktail, was an oasis of delicate femininity within the cold house and the rugged and dreary landscape. From the shade and texture of the window curtains to the small pieces of bric-a-brac casually disposed on the lamp tables and mantlepiece, one saw the loving effort of a lonely woman trying to build something permanent and beautiful in an ugly and temporary spot.

A tall Bakongo servant, impeccably dressed in white, passed the drinks on a silver tray.

"We use only Bakongo servants on purpose, to give an example of normality so to speak," she said, after the butler had left the room. "Still, since the terror, we lock the doors of our bedrooms and keep guns under the pillow. Most other Europeans in the district prefer to use reliable Bailundo servants from the south. But I am fatalistic. As you know, we were sent up here *after* the fifteenth of March. So, in a sense, I was spared the first great shock. Now, it is the waiting that is so nervewrecking."

Darkness descended rapidly over the countryside. The strong searchlight at the airstrip roamed along the barbed wire fence and beyond it to the edges of the bush, occasionally striking the windows of the living room, thus adding a kind of sinister warning to the quiet indoors. She rose to her feet to draw the window blinds and close the curtains.

"Once, by mistake, the siren went off as the light beam hit the windows," she said, as she returned to the sofa. "I was alone in the house, sitting right here on this sofa. I tried to get up, but I couldn't. I tried to reach for my glass, but I couldn't. I just sat here, half paralyzed, until the butler came in to ask me what time dinner should be served."

Presently her husband walked in with two other dinner guests. One of them was a brigadier-general, the operations commander in the northern sector, on an inspection visit to the Angola-Congo border. The other one was a youthful major, the C. O. of the special infantry battalion stationed at Maquela. The general was a dark, wiry man with a strong face and intense brown eyes, and the major, despite his youth, appeared competent and hardened by experience. But the host looked tired and disenchanted.

"The vultures are all around us," he said bitterly, as we sat down for dinner, "as vultures always are when they sense the stench of blood. Yesterday, the vultures were some of our compatriots, but they were not here when the blood bath came. Today, the vultures appear under the pious disguise of political idealists, United Nations diplomats and the like. They all share something in common: they hope to gain from the misery and blood which befell this land on the morning of March the fifteenth. Who will pay the penalty? All of us *here:* the hard-working settler, the often insulted public servant in the bush, the unknown infantry soldier forgotten in the jungle, and the masses of poor Africans who were once exploited by our kin, and are now being exploited, used and abused, in the name of black nationalism. But whatever your philosophy or your feelings, you have got to fight eye for eye, nose for nose, when the murderer knocks at the door. That is why we are staying here."

The Bakongo butler, assisted by two Bakongo servants also dressed in white and wearing clean white gloves, began to carve the roast beef methodically, with a long, sharp knife, on a carving table which he had brought close to the hostess' chair.

"This is a crazy world," the young major was saying. "In this last truckload of U.P.A. terrorists caught near Dembe, twenty-six of them, by their own admission, had been persuaded to join the U.P.A. by the offer of cabinet posts and ambassadorships to the United Nations. Two-thirds of them were completely illiterate and half of them were Congolese Bakongos who came across the border to claim their new posts! Among them was a boy, only fifteen, who was persuaded by the U.P.A. to murder his foster father, a white doctor, with the promise that he would receive the doctor's shining instruments and his diploma to practice medicine."

"Perhaps if we had given them more education, most of these horrors wouldn't have happened," the hostess put in. "Elsewhere in Angola I have always felt safer alone in the bush than walking the streets of New York or London after dark."

"You are contradicting yourself, my dear," her husband replied. "If education alone were the answer, the literate nightprowlers of New York and London should be no threat to your security. As for incentives to become a terrorist, my dear major, I believe that the prospect of disemboweling a man with a sharp knife and then raping and beheading his wife is a much greater attraction to most of these terrorists . . ."

The Bakongo butler stepped forward to the hostess' side, with a lighted match in his white-gloved hand.

"Thank you," she said, after he lit her cigarette.

". . . Yet, the most difficult thing to comprehend is the horrible atrocities they practiced on small children," the major was saying, as one of the young Bakongo waiters poured the port wine, "It seems so pointless . . . even from a terrorist's point of view."

"This is a peculiar war, indeed," the general put in, forcefully changing the tone of the conversation. "I call this operation in northern Angola the war of the captains, and by captains I mean the subaltern officers, the captains and the lieutenants. In the bush or in remote posts, the company or the platoon operates almost independently, as a guerrilla army complete in itself. So the captain or the lieutenant must often be his own general, his own chief of staff, his own logistics man, his own counsel, and even his own statesman and judge."

As I retired to my room I noticed through the window

overlooking the airstrip the lonely figure of the tall lieutenant sitting behind the wheel of a jeep. Pale moonlight
covered the countryside with a veil of quietude, but the
beam from the revolving searchlight in the tower appeared and disappeared as though it were the long arms
of a clock marking time and anxiety. I looked through the
window several times before I finally surrendered to
sleep. The young lieutenant was still there, chainsmoking
and absolutely alone. Only his head moved once in a
while, turned to a window upstairs, it seemed to me, behind which the lovely hostess was undoubtedly preparing
for bed.

At eleven o'clock the following morning, after bidding
farewell to my hostess, I walked out to my plane which
the pilot had readied for the take-off. The host accompanied me. The general was also at the airstrip. His military monoplane was about to take him to São Salvador,
another key town in the northern sector.

"The *cassimbo* has lifted in our honor," the general
said, as we shook hands. And he added, pointing at his
waiting small plane, "The only reason I joined the infantry, rather than the more glamorous air force, is that I
have always been petrified of flying machines. Nobody
has ever explained to me *satisfactorily* why these things
actually fly. But in the last few months I have spent practically half my time in the air, at treetop level. I feel like a
trapeze artist who is not quite sure whether his partner
will catch him. Oh, well . . ."

A military jeep approached us coming from the village
and the major alighted from it. He looked rather sad.

"One of my morning patrols hit a land mine right on the main road at Banza Sosso, less than a mile from the border post," the major said, addressing the general.

"Any casualties?" the general asked, as he lit a cigarette for himself and offered his package around.

"The lead jeep was blown to bits," the major answered, accepting a light from the general. "The lieutenant and the driver in it were killed instantly. The other three jeeps of the patrol escaped. My boys caught and cut down four of the terrorists, as they crossed the border. Presumably they were the ones who set up the land mine. But two others escaped to the sanctuary. I wish, sir, you would allow me once in a while to pay a visit to the terrorist sanctuary across the border."

"Major, you must resist temptation," the general said. "But if you cannot resist it, don't ever ask me in advance. . . . I must get you a replacement for the poor lieutenant."

"I feel particulary bad, sir, because this officer was not supposed to lead the patrol," the major said. "He was on duty yesterday afternoon and evening here at the airstrip. But I asked him to take the place of another officer who came down with a fever."

Instinctively I turned my head to the house. The hostess, in a bright green dress, was waving at us from the terrace.

As we prepared to board our respective planes, a weary group of soldiers emerged from the elephant grass at the turn of the dirt road. As they approached us I noticed the fatigue on their unshaven faces. Their brown-green camouflage uniforms were almost the color of mud, but they came to stiff attention in front of the two officers. Each soldier carried a submachine gun, a long bush knife, two belts of ammunition and a canteen, but the sergeant in command of the detail and the corporal also carried precision rifles, to pick up snipers at a distance. Two prisoners, barefooted and wearing dirty shorts, walked dejectedly between two soldiers, their hands tied.

"This is the detail I sent out three days ago to pick up and bring back a stubborn farmer who insisted on going back to his farm in a danger zone near Beu," the major explained to the general. And turning to the sergeant he asked, "You haven't found the farmer?"

"We found only his head stuck on a pole in front of his house, sir. We buried it. We could not find the rest of his body," the sergeant replied.

"Who are these two clowns?" the major asked, pointing at the prisoners.

"One of our informants at Cuilo Futa put the finger on them. He had seen these two coming from the farm with bags of stolen goods," the sergeant said. "I persuaded the prisoners to talk. Each one of them claims he is innocent and accuses the other of murdering the farmer."

"What would you do in a case like this, general?" the major asked.

"Do not ask me, major. You are in command here," the general said.

"I would be inclined to believe both prisoners, major," my host said. "Each one of them believes himself innocent because the U.P.A. leaders have convinced him that it is no crime to murder and mutilate a white man. And they are also right when they accuse each other of killing the farmer."

"I would go along with that reasoning, too," the general said, as he put on his dark glasses and stepped reluctantly into the cabin of the monoplane.

"Lock them up at the barracks," the major said to the sergeant. "Oh, by the way, sergeant, do not hesitate to shoot them down if they attempt to escape."

"You may rest assured, sir," the sergeant said.

"Any other encounters?"

"Yes, sir, we established contact with a small gang of terrorists in a jungle between Beu and Cuilo Futa. We killed a few. I do not know how many because the others fled taking the bodies and weapons with them. One of my men was killed and buried on the spot. I left another one behind at Cuilo Futa, suffering from dystentery."

"Very well, sergeant. Write a report. Now, take these boys to the barracks and give them some brandy and food," the major said. The sergeant gave his commanding officer a military salute and wheeled around.

"I hope to see you again," my host said as we shook hands in farewell.

After our small plane was airborne I asked the pilot to dip his wing in a salute to the charming hostess who was still standing on the terrace, the palm of her right hand raised as a shield, to protect her eyes from the sun as she waved to us with her left hand.

3

The Massacre at Quitexe

Quitexe is a village and small commercial center located about forty kilometers south of Carmona, the capital of the coffee-rich Uige district of northern Angola. On the morning of March 15, 1961, Quitexe was one of the targets of bands of terrorists who were disguised as early shoppers. The massacre, which began as the village church bells tolled eight o'clock, was one of the fastest and most horribly efficient of all the terrorist onslaughts which occurred that day all over northern Angola.

The village butcher, his wife and his daughter escaped the slaughter. Their escape was a narrow one; instinct on the part of the man must have been what saved them. Both the butcher and his pretty daughter were semiprofessional hunters and they kept an assortment of rifles and ammunition in their second-floor apartment above the shop where they sold meat and hides.

A year later I visited the man in his house at Quitexe and he described to me the terrifying events of that unforgettable morning. On the commode in the modest dining room rested an amateurish photograph of a pretty brunette with curly hair. "I have sent my girl to the south. I don't want her around here with all these soldiers . . . they are nice boys, but you understand what I mean—" he said, apologetically.

"From these two windows in this room I can see most of the houses in the village," the butcher began, pointing to specific places as he spoke, "I can see the doors of the two grocery stores, the clothing store, the pharmacy, the hardware and farming store, the gas and oil station, the trading post, the post office. We open our doors for business at eight o'clock sharp, but I get up at six every morning to feed the animals, cut the meat, sort out the fish. I always eat a heavy breakfast at seven-thirty—at least a bowl of soup, eggs and sausage, bread and coffee. I always eat well in the morning. But that morning, when my wife Maria, my daughter Lourdes and I sit down at the table for breakfast, I cannot even eat my soup! My stomach feels funny, nervous. I say to myself, 'I am not sick, why do I not eat?' My wife turns to me and says, 'Why do you not eat, man, are you sick?' . . . I am not sick but something is wrong. My daughter Lourdes says, 'It is so quiet outside!' and that is indeed funny because at seven-thirty the natives and farmers who come up from the *sanzalas* and farms to do their shopping or trade are usually talking loud and laughing in groups outside while waiting for the stores to open. I go to the window to see. There they are, as usual, the natives and a few white farmers in front of the doors of the stores. But the funny thing is that the natives are not talking loud or joking or laughing. They are kind of huddled in groups, looking sullen or talking low. Even funnier, most of them are wearing their heavy coats although the morning is warm.

"My daughter turns to me and says, 'Do you think, Papa, that they are hiding something under their coats?' ... It is now less than a quarter to eight. There is a group of eight natives in front of my door, so I stick my head outside the window and greet them. 'Good morning, boys!' and three of them raise their heads and greet me back, 'Good morning, boss!' ... But the other five are like statues. I do not see their faces, I do not know who they are. But I feel something is wrong. We have no telephone from house to house here, so I cannot warn the others. 'Papa, shall I go and warn the other stores that something may be wrong?' my daughter asks, and I whisper back to her, 'You are crazy, girl. Bring the rifles and ammunition quickly.' As I told you, sir, both Lourdes and myself are good hunters. Now it is only a few minutes before eight o'clock. I am not going to open my door.

"Lourdes and I are kneeling with our loaded rifles by

the open window, while my wife stands behind us to hold a third rifle and reload ours. I feel now that something terrible is about to happen and I am ready. The church tower strikes eight o'clock and the doors of the stores start to open and all the natives and the few white farmers walk in. My head is still outside the window but I do not show my rifle. One of the natives below raises his head, grins at me and says, 'Open the door, boss!' and I grin back and tell him, 'In a minute, boy, in a minute.'

"It is only a few minutes after eight o'clock, and all of a sudden it is like a hurricane in hell. The most awful screams from everywhere in the village! Horrible screams mostly from women and children! I figure that the terrorists started the slaughter inside the stores and in the other houses exactly at the same time. The screams are so piercing that for a moment Lourdes' and my fingers are frozen on the triggers. The natives under my window draw their machetes and scatter guns from under their coats and start yelling, '*Mata! UPA! Mata! UPA!*' and begin chopping at my door. I say to Lourdes, 'Keep cool, girl, and don't miss a shot.' In thirty seconds we blow the heads off the eight terrorists under my window. The three of them I know from around here look up at me, kind of surprised and indignant as I shoot them. They feel I have got no right to shoot them, but they have got the right to murder me and my wife and rape my daughter. It is a funny world!

"The screams become moans, fewer and fewer, because the dead do not complain anymore. A few of the victims, blood all over them, manage to run onto the street, but

the bandits go after them, yelling like crazy, and finish them off, cutting off their arms or legs or heads. It is horrible to see this from my own window. Lourdes and I are finished with the eight bandits under my window, so now we shoot at the ones chasing our people on the street. My old friend Carvalho, the farmer from Aldeia Viçosa, runs out of the hardware store. He is bleeding, he has no weapon, and two terrorists close in on him for the kill. I aim my rifle and shoot, but I miss the two bandits and hit my old friend who drops dead. I cry, 'God forgive me!' but Lourdes quickly kills both terrorists with her repeating rifle. Then I see this child, the little daughter of the clothing store, running into the street, with a big black after her. My wife cries, 'Oh, Lord, have mercy!' And then I see the Land Rover of Dr. Sousa from Carmona wheeling down the road and almost hitting the child. The doctor steps on the brakes when he sees the child, but the terrorist pays no attention to the doctor and splits open the head of the child with his machete. My wife begins to scream and my daughter is sobbing but still holding on to her rifle. The doctor gets his automatic from the glove compartment and shoots the bandit. Crazily, the doctor jumps out of the Land Rover to go toward a group of yelling terrorists coming out of the pharmacy. I yell at him, 'Doctor, get the hell out of here and give the warning at Carmona!' The doctor comes to his senses, jumps back into the Land Rover, turns around and drives away fast before the terrorists can get him.

"We have lots of ammunition, thank God. So, Lourdes and I keep on firing, we kill a few more and the others disappear behind the houses. Now everything is very quiet. I do not hear even a moan. There are only pieces of human bodies on the street and doorways of the stores, and pools of blood are everywhere. My wife and Lourdes are sobbing and I give them big glasses of brandy to steady them. I fear the terrorists are about to storm my house, so we load our guns and prepare to make them pay heavily. I swear I'll kill my wife and my daughter before the beasts get their hands on them. But everything stays very quiet. I wait. Maria and Lourdes are now saying the rosary and weeping while I keep my watch by the window. Nine o'clock comes and the church bell does not toll. The big birds are flying overhead and I shoot at them to scatter them away. I wait. The terrorists do not come back to my house. Around noon a platoon of soldiers arrives from Carmona. It is much too late for the dead."

4

The Battle of Carmona

Oh, evil night,
For whom lie you in wait?
For the poor soldiers
And the shepherds of flocks
And the men of the sea,
What will you grant them?
CAMOENS (1524-1580)

CARMONA, the capital of the Uige District in northern Angola, is a modern and well-planned town which could be found in the American southwest or in southern Europe. It is forty-odd kilometers north of Quitexe and rests comfortably on a small and fertile plateau, surrounded by the greenery of a pleasant valley and the rolling hills beyond. It was practically born with the coffee boom in northern Angola, and it nearly faced extinction on that fateful day of March 15, 1961.

It was nearly ten o'clock in the morning of that day when a dozen customers, enjoying their morning coffee on the veranda of the Grande Hotel do Uige, were rudely shaken by the stormy arrival of a careening Land Rover which shot into town from the Quitexe Road. The driver was Dr. Sousa, a civic leader of Carmona, a normally calm person, sixty years of age, with a leathery face, disorderly grey hair and penetrating brown eyes. He slammed on the brakes as he approached the Grande Hotel and shouted at the sleepy group on the veranda, "To your guns! And lock your doors! Terrorism has broken out! I'm going to the governor!"

Before those on the veranda had a chance to digest the warning, Dr. Sousa was off to the sidewalk cafe further up the main avenue.

"To your guns! Terrorists are coming!" he shouted at the perplexed patrons at the sidewalk tables. He did not stop again until he reached the governor's mansion at the end of the avenue.

"Is the doctor out of his mind?" asked one man.

"I have no gun. What is he talking about?" asked a second.

"He said terrorists. Where? What terrorists?" exclaimed a third.

"We may as well find out what is going on," said the first one, and the group from the sidewalk café began to walk in the direction of the governor's mansion. At the same time most of the customers from the veranda of the Grande Hotel began to head slowly in the same direction.

When the two groups merged at the gates of the mansion they were joined by others, mostly men and boys, but the two stern *cypaio* sentries, native soldiers of the regular infantry company stationed at Carmona, barred the entrance with crossed bayonets.

"What is going on?" asked a bystander.

"Dr. Sousa said something about terrorism. Maybe it

was a fight between Bakongos and Bailundos. They hate each other's guts," ventured one of the café customers.

"Who knows? Maybe the United Nations has invaded Angola," another bystander speculated, half-seriously. Some of the spectators laughed, but others made grimaces; no one seemed particularly alarmed. The crowd lingered about the gate, attracting newcomers, and some of them speculated wildy on the reasons for the doctor's panic.

Presently, a military jeep, traveling even faster than Dr. Sousa's Land Rover, rounded the big post office building, shot through the crowd and came to a stop at the gate.

"What is going on, captain?" several voices shouted.

"I don't know," the officer replied as he dashed through the gate.

Hardly a minute elapsed before the governor's secretary, a pleasant young man with a boyish face, emerged and climbed to the front seat of the jeep. Someone grabbed his sleeve.

"What on earth is going on?" he asked.

"Let go of my sleeve, man! Terrorism has broken out in the country. But keep calm. A few of you run to the churches and ask the priests to toll the alarm. On to the barracks, driver."

Half the crowd dispersed quickly, some going to the churches, others hurrying home to their families. Minutes later a motorcyclist arrived at great speed.

"Do you know anything, senhor?" asked an anxious bystander.

"Yes," the motorcyclist answered, as he removed his

goggles, "an amateur radio operator near Nova Caipemba has been flashing a message and I just caught it on my short wave set. There has been a massacre at Nova Caipemba this morning. I must see the governor at once, corporal."

"I will take you in," the corporal of the guard said, opening the gate.

Suddenly the crowd began to realize that something frightening was happening around them. Faces became tense and eyes somber.

"But Dr. Sousa was not coming from Nova Caipemba. He arrived from the Quitexe road," said a boy in the crowd.

"Maybe the doctor saw something toward Quitexe," said another boy.

"How far is Nova Caipemba from here?" someone asked.

"About one hundred kilometers," another one answered.

"Well, that gives us a little time. They are probably walking through the bush."

"What guaranty do you have that it will be the same ones?"

Dr. Sousa emerged from the governor's mansion, a worried look on his face.

"Is it bad, doctor?" a woman asked.

"I am afraid it may be very bad," the doctor answered. Then, he raised his voice to reach everyone in the crowd. "Now, you people, I suggest that you leave your women and children locked up at home, get whatever weapons you have, and join me in the gymnasium as soon as possible. We have to organize some kind of civilian brigade, and quickly, because there are so few soldiers here . . . The ones living on the edge of town had better bring their women and children to the gymnasium and the radio station. Pass the word."

As the doctor headed for his Land Rover the churches of Carmona began to toll the alarm and the spines of the people began to shiver.

Dr. Sousa drove now at a moderate pace along the well-paved streets of Carmona, past the cement buildings with their balconies fragrant with vases of sweet basil and violets. He saw the curious and frightened faces of women as they began to understand the meaning of the church bells. Presently the doctor stopped his car in front of the last house on a dead end street in the eastern part of town. The house was a comfortable two-story building of masonry, a mixture of nineteenth-century colonial and provincial Portuguese which included a wide stone stairway from the ground to the veranda on the second floor and a well-tended garden on the side of the house. The road east to Negage could be seen from the windows.

His son, a dark young man of thirty, wearing a physician's white coat, was waiting at the door.

"Why are the bells ringing so insistently? A big fire?" the younger Sousa asked.

"Do you still have any patients in the office?" his father asked.

"No, I just got rid of the last one."

"The servants?"

"They're gone after the bells, I believe."

"All right, Pedro. Take off your white coat, get your rifle and ammunition, bring your own car and join me at the gymnasium."

"What goes on, father? . . . You were gone to Quitexe early this morning!"

"I was, son. And as I entered the village the terrorists began slaughtering everybody in sight, including the children. I barely had time to turn around and drive back here to give the alarm. I'm going to collect my own rifle and automatic." Without a word, Dr. Pedro followed his father into the house.

Fifteen minutes later the senior doctor joined his son and a few other men at the door of the radio station which was located across the street from the Grande Hotel. The hotel veranda was now empty, as were the sidewalk tables of the café; several civilians carrying weapons were walking rapidly towards the gymnasium.

"You go into the station, Pedro," Dr. Sousa told his son, "and tell the girl announcer to give periodic warnings . . . ask people to lock doors and windows and be on the alert."

Then the doctor drove his Land Rover up the main avenue past the governor's mansion, and came to a stop in front of the large C.T.T. post, telegraph and telephone building. Inside, a few people appeared to be glued to the main counter, their anxious eyes on the two employees who seemed either inscrutable or ignorant of what was going on. Dr. Sousa walked directly into the office of the postmaster, a middle-aged man with completely white hair.

"Well?" the doctor asked.

"The telephone and the telegraph lines have been cut," the postmaster announced somberly. "We finally got Luanda on the wireless. Very bad connection. But here it is . . . Our airstrip is completely closed by ground fog which is covering the entire plateau. Luanda cannot land any reinforcements here today, even if they had them. They say they will try tomorrow . . . if we are still here. We asked them to drop paratroopers on the Negage valley where the fog is not so bad. They say they have no paratroopers; they are going to ask Lisbon for some, but this will take a couple of days, at best. In other words, today the only thing we can get from Luanda is their sympathy."

"So, that is it!" Dr. Sousa exclaimed, shaking his head.

"That is it, I am afraid," the postmaster concurred.

"Any new reports?" the doctor asked.

"A report of other attacks at Nambuangongo and Buela, but no details," the postmaster said. "Was it bad at Quitexe, doctor?"

"Sickening. They must have attacked as the stores opened at eight o'clock. When I arrived in the village, they were dragging the bodies onto the little square and cutting them to pieces with their machetes. It will be a miracle if anybody at Quitexe escaped that massacre."

"Oh, God!" cried the postmaster, and crossed himself.

It was noon when the doctor walked into the gymnasium which was filled with several hundred men and teenage boys armed with an assortment of weapons—from modern repeating rifles and automatic pistols to ancient hunting rifles, machetes, and even swords and native spears with bayonets. Some of the enterprising teen-agers had tied native *catanas* with wire to the tips of wooden poles, making a kind of lance. Outside the gymnasium two or three hundred more people, similarly armed, lingered about amid an array of vehicles which ranged from open lorries to jeeps and small sports cars. Perhaps half the crowd had firearms: the improvised weapons of the other half would be only as effective as the recklessness of their bearers.

Dr. Sousa elbowed his way to the stage where a *colono* was haranguing the crowd. The doctor became aware that the mood of his fellow *colonos* was an angry one. It was directed against the governor-general in Luanda and the government in Lisbon for having neglected the defense of northern Angola against the possibility of just such a terrorist onslaught, particularly in the light of what had been happening next door in the Congo. There were scattered shouts of "death" and "down" to the rulers they considered responsible for their predicament.

"We begged time and again for modern weapons to keep in our homes, as a kind of militia—and what happened? Luanda and Lisbon ignored us. We begged time and again for a strong military garrison—and what happened?"

Dr. Sousa pushed the orator away from the microphone.

"All this is true, and I should know it better than anybody else," the doctor began, as the shouts from the audience quieted down. "But I did not ask you to come here for a debate. We may have little time left and we must brace ourselves for our own defense. There are five thousand of us in Carmona and only a company of soldiers—"

"No more, doctor, no more!" the previous speaker interrupted loudly, waiving his arms. "The captain and the first platoon are now driving north to Nova Caipemba, and a lieutenant and a second platoon have been dispatched south towards Quitexe. Only the sentries at the governor's mansion are left!"

Dr. Sousa was speechless for a few seconds.

"It is not possible!" he finally exclaimed.

"I saw the lorries and jeeps with my own eyes!" protested the other man. Several shouts from the audience confirmed the report.

With great difficulty the doctor restored order in the noisy audience.

"No matter, we must remain calm and brace ourselves for the attack," the doctor began, as the crowd again deferred to him. "I am not a general, but I suggest a plan as follows. . . . The best marksmen with rifles take positions in the upstairs windows of the stronger houses along the edges of town. All women, except the ones who have rifles and are good shots, and children should be kept here in the gymnasium and in the warehouse. All the other men and boys form motorized patrols. Open lorries and Land Rovers are the best cars, I think. Fill all the tanks with gasoline. When they come, do not wait for them. Go toward them and kill them as fast as you can. Remember, *they* will not spare you or your women or your children. When the attack starts, all the church bells must toll as loudly as possible. The noise may confuse some of us, but it will confuse them even more, I am sure. When they set fire to a house, do not waste your time trying to stop the fire. Your business is to kill terrorists, not to save property. When this is over, it is better to have a burned town and people still living than a preserved town with nothing but our dead bodies in it!"

"The drums!" someone shouted at the door of the gymnasium.

The grim crowd began to evacuate the gymnasium in orderly fashion. It was one o'clock in the afternoon, and the clouds were still hanging low over Carmona.

Dr. Pedro joined his father in the Land Rover. The monotonous call of the drums—there must have been hundreds of them—came from the hills north and northwest of Carmona, from the tall elephant grass in the valley east of the town, and from the forest to the south along the Quitexe road, and it reached their ears like the sinister overture of a Wagnerian opera about to be staged in the heart of Africa. The church bells of Carmona were now silent, but the roar of automobile and lorry engines filled the street. Dr. Sousa headed the Land Rover up the street in the direction of the military barracks, and he turned on the radio.

"Any chance that we may be heard *anywhere?*" Dr. Pedro asked, as he quietly polished his rifle with a suede cloth.

"Not a chance, son. The radius of our transmitter is twenty or thirty kilometers, if that much, and we do not have a short wave transmitter," the older Dr. Sousa said.

"But we will be heard by the fellows beating the drums around Carmona. Many of them have transistor radios."

The sweet, delicately feminine voice of the disc jockey was coming through like a timid solo against the menacing background of the still distant drums.

". . . I shall repeat this warning and other flashes at periodic intervals," she was confiding to the microphone. "Next, you will hear the inimitable voice of your and my favorite, the great Amalia, queen of the *fado* . . ." But then she suddenly interrupted herself. "The station has just learned that practically the entire company of soldiers stationed at Carmona has been sent—"

"Christ Almighty!" swore the doctor, as he slammed on the brakes and turned off the radio. "That girl is telling the enemy that we are even weaker than they think. Pedro, you run back to the station and tell her to send out an immediate flash announcing that a battalion of paratroopers is on the way from Luanda and is about to be dropped here, and have her repeat the flash several times. Then pass the word quietly that it is not true, otherwise the vigilantes may become overconfident."

Pedro grabbed his rifle and jumped off the Land Rover, and the senior Dr. Sousa continued to the barracks which were located two blocks from his house, near the Negage road. He found the first-sergeant, a robust man of about forty, with intelligent but tough features, at the entrance.

"I was about to go and look for you, doctor," the first sergeant said, as he leaned his elbow on the door of the car.

"What on earth was the idea of sending the two platoons away where the damage has already been done, and leaving this town naked?" the doctor asked, lighting a cigarette for himself and offering one to the soldier.

"It was not the captain's idea, nor was it the lieutenant's or mine. You know, doctor . . ."

"What have you got here?"

"Apart from the European corporal and the four *cypaios* at the governor's," the first sergeant answered, "I have myself and eighteen soldiers, ten of them African."

The doctor whistled with apprehension.

"How reliable are your ten African soldiers?" he asked.

"Quite reliable, I believe," the first sergeant said. "Not a single one of them is a Bakongo. Four of them, without uniforms, I have sent out in the bush to scout the enemy. They should return within an hour, I hope."

"Can you spare any guns for my vigilantes?"

"Not many, doctor, maybe four rifles and a couple of revolvers."

They appraised each other in silence for a few seconds.

"Antonio, you are a professional soldier and you have been around a long time. What do you honestly think our chances are?" the doctor asked, looking the first sergeant in the eyes.

Antonio wrinkled his forehead, scratched his chin, thoughtfully, cleared his throat, spat, rubbed the heel of his boot on the saliva, and finally looked straight at the doctor.

"Nil," he replied curtly.

The doctor had to swallow twice before he recovered the power of speech.

"That is encouraging," he said finally. "But you ought to know. Do you mind letting me in on your reasoning?"

The first sergeant cleared his throat again and switched the strap of his submachine gun from the right to the left shoulder.

"I estimate the Bakongo mob over the hills, in the *capim* of the valley, and in the bush," Antonio began, his outstretched hand pointing successively to three cardinal points, "I estimate them as close to twenty thousand, maybe more. Most of them are not worth much as fighters, but by the time they attack they will be doped up, drunk with *aguardente,* or their bodies rubbed with *milongo* by the witch doctors to make them believe they are immune to our bullets. So, no matter how many we kill, they will keep on coming until they overrun us by sheer numbers."

"And nobody will live to tell the tale!" Dr. Sousa remarked, lighting another cigarette with a hand which was no longer steady.

"You have it about right, doctor," the soldier said, calmly, accepting another cigarette. "But I hope I am wrong. And we have to go on from there."

"What about your soldiers, Antonio?"

"That is what I wanted to see you about, doctor. I figure the thing this way, doctor. The U.P.A. organization must have given a great deal of thought to this thing. After all, Carmona is the capital of the district. If they take it, the rest of northern Angola will crumble. Carmona has probably the brightest street lights of any African town. These neon lights on the streets make the night as bright as day. I believe their first target will be the electric power station. I believe that I and my soldiers should barricade ourselves in the station and keep the lights going for you vigilantes as long as possible. I do not mean that this Bakongo mob fights well in the dark. They do not. What I mean, doctor, is that the U.P.A. fellows in Leo, who think that Carmona is a kind of fortress, must have realized that our defense in total darkness would be absolutely impossible. We would end up by shooting each other. Understand me, doctor?"

"I do, Antonio, and I agree that you should take up the power station."

They shook hands solemnly and the doctor continued on his way. As he turned a corner, he saw three truck-loads of people, men, women and children, parked in front of a tavern and restaurant. The tavern keeper, a typical *colono* with a barrel chest and hard features, in shirt sleeves and carrying a rifle in the sling over his shoulder, was arguing irately with three men, all of them wearing coats and hats, obviously the leaders of the three truckloads of people.

"Come here, doctor," the tavern keeper called out. "These people are about to desert the ship. They heard that the road to Negage is still open. Apparently, a driver arrived from Negage an hour ago and said that he saw no terrorists. I am telling them that they are cowardly—"

The doctor alighted from the Land Rover and joined the group.

"There are three roads out of Carmona," he said slowly, addressing the three men who tipped their hats as he approached. "We know that the road south to Quitexe and the road northwest to Songo and Nova Caipemba are occupied by terrorists. As yet, we do not know whether they have cut off the road east to Negage. But if they were not there when your driver came through, they may be there already. Listen to the drums, they are all around us. . . . You are leading your families into a sure slaughter. You are being stupid, if not cowardly. Stay with your neighbors. That is the only thing you have left."

Some of the women were weeping, but the children were playing with each other and seemed quite unconcerned.

"Let us stay!" some of the women cried out from the truck. The three men were still hesitant. Impulsively, Dr. Sousa drew his automatic from the holster and pointed the muzzle straight at the men.

"If you want to leave, by God, you leave," he said, sternly. "But those women and children are staying. They would not have a chance on the road."

"Have we got any chance here, doctor?" the most stubborn of the three men asked in return.

"Yes, we have, for as long as we fight," the doctor replied firmly. Deep in his heart he could not bring himself to agree with the first sergeant's verdict.

"The doctor is absolutely right," the tavern keeper said.

The three men shook their heads in doubt but returned to their vehicles and ordered the drivers to turn around.

"I will be up there on the roof, with my brother and cousin," the *colono* said to the doctor, as he pointed to the terrace roof of his establishment. "We all have rifles."

The doctor shook hands with the tavern keeper and wished him good luck.

On his way down the main avenue he turned on the radio. The announcer was now trustfully forecasting the imminent arrival of reinforcements.

". . . a whole regiment of paratroopers has now reached the skies of the Uige, and those brave soldiers are about to be dropped from the skies into the valley of Carmona to punish the terrorists. But, in the meantime, it is important to keep our alert in town, for the terrorists may strike at any moment. . . ."

Dr. Sousa turned off the radio. The vehicles of the vigilantes were now patrolling every street, driving along very slowly, the faces of the men and boys very tense and grim. As he looked at the upper windows and roofs of some of the houses, the doctor saw the muzzles of waiting rifles. The drumming in the hills and in the valley had not changed its monotone, but it sounded closer to the outskirts of town.

The doctor stopped his Land Rover at the door of the Grande Hotel, and his son, who was talking to a group of vigilantes across the street, came over to join him.

"I think I will take my own car with four other men. The Mercedes is quite sturdy and I can use it as a tank," Pedro said, as he readjusted the ammunition belt around his waist.

"Good idea, Pedro," the senior doctor said.

They went in together and found the professional white hunter and his wife busily removing the grease from their hunting guns.

"We had all our guns greased and crated to take off for Luanda tomorrow on a vacation, and now this thing happens," the hunter remarked, in disgust.

Dr. Sousa sat down and beckoned the waiter to bring coffee and cognac for everyone. He looked up at the wall clock in the dining room. It was five minutes past three o'clock. He set his own wrist watch by it.

"My wrist watch always stops when I get emotional about something," Dr. Sousa complained.

"I am very nervous myself. I am so relieved that our children are in Luanda," the woman said, without taking her eyes from the task of ungreasing the guns.

"Jacinto, you know the Bakongo mind better than anybody else," Pedro said, addressing the professional hunter. "What do you think?"

"About what? If you mean, who are they, the answer is, many of them are from the District, and perhaps just as many are Congolese from across the border. It is the same tribe, as you know. The U.P.A. fellows from Leo must have organized this thing carefully, but I believe that only a minority of the mob will have firearms. Most of them will attack with *catanas*. By the way, my own gunbearer has joined them. He is a rat and always plays the winning side. He thinks we are done for."

"When will they attack?" Pedro insisted.

"They are working themselves up to it, slowly, as the Bakongo mind goes," the hunter answered. "Then, they go wild and blind, so to speak. I would say that they will not approach the town until sunset."

"There is no sun today," the doctor commented.

"I mean, until darkness."

"Will you stay here at the hotel, Jacinto?" Dr. Sousa asked.

"I have organized a small group of sharpshooters," the hunter replied. "We will take positions in the back windows of the hotel. The *capim* is only a hundred yards away, and they are sure to come through there."

"I have spoken to the first sergeant," the doctor said, "and he is very pessimistic. How do you feel, Jacinto?"

"How do I feel, doctor? Scared, naturally. Will they overrun us? Surely, if they keep on coming. There must be more than thirty thousand of those clowns on the hills and in the valley. But the human wave may break and turn back if we kill enough of them and fast enough."

Dr. Sousa and his son shook hands with the white hunter and his wife and left the hotel. Outside they separated to organize their respective patrols.

"Get something to eat, Pedro. The vigil may go on all night," the doctor told his son as they parted. Pedro nodded and waved *au revoir* to his father.

Driving up the main avenue again Dr. Sousa could not resist the temptation of turning on the radio.

"It is impossible to answer all the telephone calls flooding the station," the disc jockey was saying. "We do expect a terrorist attack late this afternoon or evening, but the attackers will be destroyed. The troops and the vigilantes have taken their positions and are constantly patrolling the edge of town. There is, practically, a machinegun on every roof of Carmona and enough ammunition to hold back an army. The first battalion of paratroopers has landed in the valley and is now progressing toward the hills. More battalions are expected shortly. The governor-general is flying in from Luanda to direct the defense of Carmona . . ."

The first sergeant, with a native soldier at the wheel, was coming down the street and he stopped his jeep to palaver with the doctor. He also had his radio on.

"Doctor, I am afraid the radio announcer may have to go to purgatory for lying so much," the sergeant remarked.

"Any news from your scouts, Antonio?"

"Yes, doctor. Three of them have just returned. They estimate the Bakongo mob at thirty thousand or more, poorly armed, thank God. Many of them, my scouts say, are already drunk and doped, and that is bad, because then they will not care. My fourth scout is missing. He was either caught or has joined the terrorists. Anything can happen. Good-bye, doctor. I am going to round up my boys and take up positions at the power station."

When the doctor returned to the gymnasium to enlist five vigilantes for his own patrol, it was four o'clock in the afternoon. Some of the men were stuffing their ears with absorbent cotton to filter the call of the drums.

"This drumming is driving me insane," one of the vigilantes said.

"I find it relaxing," said another one. "It makes you feel that you are just watching the cinema."

"I do not believe they will attack at all," said a third one.

"When are the reinforcements coming, doctor?" asked the first one, with cotton in his ears.

"Are you joking, *colono?*" said the second vigilante.

One could not tell that the sun had set, for the low clouds were still hanging over the cupolas of the churches. But, suddenly, it was dark and humid, and the neon street lights were turned on. Carmona became a brightly lit stage of anxiety under a roof of darkness and surrounded by a chorus of promised death. The hundreds of drums were apparently descending from the hills and worming their way through the elephant grass of the valley for the insanely monotonous beat was growing closer and closer to the hearts of the trapped *colonos*. It was deafening. Suddenly, the hills to the north and northwest of town became festive with hundreds of fires, some large, some small, which cast a macabre semicircle of orange and red shadows across the low clouds, as though in mockery of the white neon glow over the buildings and the beseiged citizens. It was eight o'clock in the evening.

Then, another sound of death was heard: thousands of voices, eerie voices coming from the night and the trees and the tall grass, chanted in unison, incessantly, the maddening cry, "*Mata! UPA! Mata! UPA!*" This was the bloody warning of the terrorists . . . Kill! UPA! Kill! UPA! . . . and the chant went on and on.

The vigilantes on the roofs trained their guns, and the patrols in vehicles along the streets on the edges of town stopped their cars but kept the engines going, the beams of their headlights pointing through the night at the still invisible terrorists. At the power station the first sergeant and his handful of soldiers waited tensely, fingers on triggers. Antonio himself rested his left hand on a switch which would turn on the spotlights as soon as the attackers got within comfortable range of the machine gun, submachine guns and rifles. He had also placed boxes of dynamite in the control room, with the purpose of blowing up a sizable number of attackers, the defenders and the building itself, should the terrorists break through into the station.

In the center of town, in the gymnasium and warehouse, the women prayed, some weeping, some with dry eyes. The older children sat tensely by their mothers, but the very young ones played unconcernedly with each other. Some of the women, with stouter hearts, were on the roofs and at the windows with their men.

Dr. Sousa and his patrol were now waiting, with many other cars, at the south end of town where the Quitexe road began.

"Any minute now," said one of Dr. Sousa's vigilantes, as he lit a cigarette and rested his rifle temporarily on his lap.

"*Mata! UPA! Mata! UPA!*" hummed, unconsciously, a second vigilante, as though he could not resist the chorus from the trees below.

"Shut up and watch your aim," snapped a third man in the Land Rover.

"Any minute now," the doctor said, echoing the first vigilante. Suddenly, he felt very calm. He knew well the temper of his tough *colonos*, and he knew that when the issue was as fundamental as this, each vigilante would dispatch a good handful of Bakongos before he met his Maker.

Abruptly, an uproar of screams and yells, punctuated methodically by the stacatto of machinegun fire, came to their ears from the north end of town, and the church bells began to toll in the highest possible key, partially drowning the monotone of the drums and the chorus of voices in the trees.

"They must be attacking the power station," said the first vigilante.

"Any minute now," said Dr. Sousa, his keen eyes on the Quitexe road ahead.

The first sergeant was right. The first wave emerged from the night, entered the orbit of the spotlights, which he turned on when the first lines were but thirty yards away, and tried to storm the station as though its walls were made of cardboard. The deadly fire from the machine gun, the submachine guns and rifles of the seventeen soldiers, cut them down in droves as they advanced. But they kept on, yelling and shooting their *canhangulos* and hunting rifles, without hitting anyone, and they continued to fall over the bodies of the men already fallen, until there was practically a wall of dead bodies around the station. At length they retreated into the elephant grass for regroupment. The first sergeant turned off the switch of the spotlights and wiped his forehead with a red handkerchief.

"Anybody hurt?" he asked.

"Nobody," answered the native corporal, a Bailundo.

"Half of the soldiers take a smoke, while the other half watches. Then the other half smokes," he ordered, as he lit a cigarette for himself. He looked at his wrist watch. The first attack, disorganized and clumsy as it was, lasted twenty minutes; there must have been well over two hundred bodies lying across the narrow battlefield.

"Sergeant," said a European corporal, "my F.B.P. will go bad after three hundred shots. What do I use then?"

"I lied to Dr. Sousa," said the sergeant. "I have four more subs in reserve in that crate. Take one when yours burns out."

Dr. Sousa's eyes were beginning to hurt from watching the narrow line of the Quitexe road, and his throat was drying up from chain smoking.

"Any minute now," Dr. Sousa said again.

"I wish the bastards would come. This waiting drives me mad," said one of the vigilantes.

"Perhaps they will not dare," another vigilante said, hopefully. "The lights are still on. Antonio and his soldiers must have beaten them at the power station."

At that moment, the yells and screams and stacatto sound of the guns came from the north end of town. The vigilantes in Dr. Sousa's Land Rover sat tensely, some watching the dark countryside ahead, the others watching the neon lights of Carmona. Five, ten, fifteeen minutes passed as the drums, the chorus of *"Mata! UPA! Mata! UPA!"* the church bells and the guns at the power station, seemed to blend harmoniously into a pattern of musical madness. Then, as suddenly as it had started, the sound from the power station halted again. The lights of Carmona were still on. The vigilantes took a deep breath of relief.

"Any minute now," said one of the vigilantes.

"Can't you say something else?" snapped the doctor. The vigilante stared at him, in perplexity.

The uproar of battle suddenly reached their ears from another direction—the east end of town. They heard distinctly the shouts of the vigilantes, "*Mata! Mata!*" which in their anger they borrowed from the attackers, as they charged upon them. Dr. Sousa and his companions heard the blazing of the guns from the roofs and windows, the yells of fury and the screams of pain, and they saw smaller bands of terrorists emerging from the night, carrying bags full of rocks which they threw at the street lights. A few of the lights were smashed, but the guns in the windows and on the roofs and from the speeding cars, were mowing down the carriers of the hand artillery as quickly as they moved into the orbit of light.

There was a wide open area at the south end of town, where Dr. Sousa and dozens of other vehicles of vigilantes were stationed. Suddenly, the elephant grass a hundred yards from their eyes began to move.

"Here they are! May the Lord have mercy on my soul," murmured a vigilante, next to Dr. Sousa, as he crossed himself.

The human wave surged from the tall grass onto the open ground and up the Quitexe road, yelling, "*Mata! UPA! Mata! UPA!,*" and waving their weapons—hunting rifles, homemade scatter guns, or *canhangulos,* a few pistols, but mostly the sharp, deadly *catanas* which resemble battle sabres. The wave in front was made up of the ones who were doped or drunk; the more sober ones marched behind the cannon fodder.

"Drive into them!" shouted Dr. Sousa at the top of his lungs as soon as the wave reached the open ground.

With the engines roaring and the guns blazing, the vehicles of the defenders drove into the mass of the attackers, but when finally the wheels were blocked by the piles of dead bodies, the vigilantes jumped out from the open trucks, jeeps and cars, yelling, "*Mata! Mata!*" and they killed right and left, with the uncontrollable ferocity of angry trapped men. Many of them fell dead in the barbarous hand-to-hand combat, but the damage they caused to the surging wave was such that the attack became completely disorganized less than fifteen minutes after it started. For a moment, the attack seemed to teeter idiotically, then it crumbled like a deck of cards. The remnants of the wave retreated back to the elephant grass, still crying "*Mata! UPA!*" but with less vigor, less conviction, and, above all, with many voices lost, for they had left hundreds of dead or dying on the open ground. The vigilantes regrouped and backed the undamaged vehicles to their original position.

Dr. Sousa, who had been fighting and killing, with an automatic in his right hand and a butcher knife in the left, returned to his Land Rover and wiped away the blood which had sprinkled on his hands and face. Then, he looked around for his team—three were back with him, two were gone.

"Do you think they will try again, doctor?" asked one of the vigilantes.

"They will," the doctor answered.

They could still hear the noise of battle from the ground behind the Grande Hotel and from the east end of town, but it had decreased in intensity. The chorus of "*Mata! UPA!*" coming from a distance behind the trees was still filling the air, and the church bells of Carmona were still tolling stridently, but the drums had died down and the fires on the hills were withering. The lights of Carmona were still shining, despite the many dark spots caused by broken bulbs.

A jeep, with four vigilantes in it, sped down the avenue and came to a screeching stop by the doctor's Land Rover.

"We beat them twice at the east end," the driver of the jeep said, "and there are so many dead piled up that it makes you sick. Dr. Pedro was killed. Are you all right here?"

"So far, yes," one of the vigilantes in the Land Rover answered. The jeep sped away again, up the avenue. Dr. Sousa pretended that he had not heard the message about his son.

Presently, there was no longer any noise of battle from any part of town. The street lights were still on and the church bells interrupted their tolling. The drums were silent. Only the chorus from the trees continued its chant.

They waited.

Around midnight the last attack came, once more from three directions—against the power station, and from the east and south. But it was clumsy and disorganized. Only the odds were frightening. Again, the vigilantes attacked the attackers, instead of waiting for their onslaught and, as the church bells resumed their desperate tolling, the last attack crumbled hopelessly and the trapped *colonos* became then the chasers, going after the routed terrorists into the tall grass and the night, crying, *"Mata! Mata!"* and killing with renewed ferocity until they became lost themselves, or recovered their senses in time to return.

The church bells halted their tolling. The town became almost silent. Only the chorus from the trees was still sending its sinister message to the tired vigilantes.

Then, a torrential rain—quite unusual in March— began to pour over Carmona and the countryside, a torrent that poured incessantly until dawn, wiping the blood from the ground and from the grass, and transforming the roads and the fields into pools of mud, and drowning completely the chorus from the trees. The weird battle of Carmona was over.

When the rain stopped and the sun rose, the sleepless vigilantes collected the bodies of their fallen neighbors to give them proper burial in the cemetry, and they opened long and deep trenches in the *capim* outside of town to bury the piles of dead bodies left by the attackers. No one bothered to count them.

5

The Sawmill at Luvo

The macabre story of Luvo—a village border post between Angola and the Republic of the Congo, not far from the Congolese river port of Matadi—was heard but not really publicized immediately after that morning of horrors. It came to outside attention for the first time through a front page story in the French newspaper, Le Monde, on July 5, 1961, in the form of an interview by a journalist, Pierre de Vos, with leaders of the U.P.A. organization in Leopoldville.

Less than a year later, when I visited the diamond mining territory of Lunda, near the Katanga border, I met by accident the weather-bitten truck driver who had arrived at Luvo at dawn on the fifteenth of March.

As we sipped mugs of beer at the bar of a tavern in Saurimo, the gateway to the huge mining concession of Diamang, he told me, with great emotion and sweeping gestures, of his adventures. The story that follows was reconstructed from the notes I made at the time, as well as from reports of other men who had not actually seen the slaughter themselves.

IN THE afternoon of March 14, 1961, Zacharias and his Kimbundo helper, Inhaca, arrived in the small town of São Salvador with a truckload of canned foodstuffs which they had brought from the costal town of Ambrizete, a small port more than halfway between Luanda and the estuary of the Congo River. After they had unloaded the shipment at the warehouse, Zacharias was told that there would be a cargo of empty wood crates for his truck to take on the return trip to Ambrizete—that is, if he cared to pick up the freight at the sawmill of Luvo which is a border village nearly forty miles to the north of São Salvador. Zacharias was pleased with the news.

"Boy, let us get on the road again, and we will get to Luvo in time for supper," the driver said, turning to his helper.

"Let us not, boss. We will never make it in daylight,

and the road is very bad," Inhaca suggested, urgently. They had been on the road for ten long hours.

"Let us toss a coin," Zacharias suggested.

"All right, boss," Inhaca agreed.

Zacharias tossed the coin and he won easily. He always carried one coin with two heads and another one with two tails.

Halfway between São Salvador and Luvo, Zacharias began to regret his victory. The narrow, dirt road was in terrible condition due to the recent rains. Presently, it was nightfall and Zacharias' kidneys and endurance gave up and he stopped the truck on a clearing by the road.

"Well, Inhaca, I guess you should have won the toss," he admitted.

"I guess I should have, boss," the Kimbundo agreed.

"We will sleep here and get back on the road before the dawn breaks," the driver said, as he left the cab to stretch his legs.

"I guess we will, boss," the helper agreed.

They shared a modest supper of bread and cheese and wine, supplies which the normally cautious Zacharias always carried in a tin box, after which they wrapped themselves in their respective blankets and went to sleep in the now empty trailer. Sometime before dawn they awakened and continued the journey.

Dawn was breaking when they arrived at Luvo, the village border post. They saw the two sleepy border guards, in their khaki uniforms, and waved to them, but they turned off to the sawmill before they reached the checkpoint. The road would go on into the Congo, to Thysville and Leopoldville.

The night watchman at the sawmill was still on duty, although the sun was rising, and he yawned and stretched his arms sleepily when the truck came to a stop.

"My name is Zacharias and this is my helper, Inhaca. I understand there is a load for Ambrizete," Zacharias said, as he alighted from the cab and offered a smoke to the night watchman who accepted it after he had readjusted the sling of his rifle.

"The crates are at the end of the yard. You can drive your trailer around and park it behind the crates," the watchman said. "The boys should be here soon and they will load your trailer the first thing."

"How are things up here?" the driver asked, to make idle conversation.

"I do not like it, but there is nothing I can do," the watchman said.

"What do you mean?" Zacharias asked, sincerely puzzled.

"Something funny is going on, but I do not know what it is. Nobody in the village does," the watchman answered. "Yesterday, a few of us went to the chief of post and told him that something funny was going on and that we were worried, and he asked, 'what?' and we could not answer, so he just shrugged his shoulders."

"Well, what is this funny thing that is going on up here?" Zacharias insisted, his curiosity increasing.

"Driver, I do not know," the watchman said, wrinkling

his forehead. "But something is not right. About half of the boys—they are all Bakongos—did not show up for work the last two days. And many of the other Bakongos around the village have been giving you a kind of funny look. And I have seen in the last few days a number of well-dressed blacks I have not seen around here before."

"Well, maybe they are planning a robbery or something—" Zacharias said, but he was interrupted by a sudden commotion in the village—yells, screams and a few rifle shots.

"Something funny is happening in the village," the watchman said, with some panic. "I must take a look." He removed the rifle from his shoulder and, carrying it in his hand, ran towards the village.

"I do not like it, boss," Inhaca said. "Let us hide the truck in the back of the yard."

Zacharias hesitated, but he decided to follow the Kimbundo's advice, this time without tossing a coin.

"It must be a robbery. None of our business, anyhow," the driver said, as he climbed back in the cab.

As they parked the truck in the back of the storage yard, behind the piles of wood crates, the sounds in the village reached their ears—frightful and piercing screams. Zacharias began to feel, with a premonition of horror, that this might be more than a case of robbery. They made a perilous climb to the top of a pile of crates from which they could see part of the village as well as the rest of the yard and the open side of the mill.

Their eyes could not believe what they saw. A crowd of yelling, shouting and laughing blacks were dragging

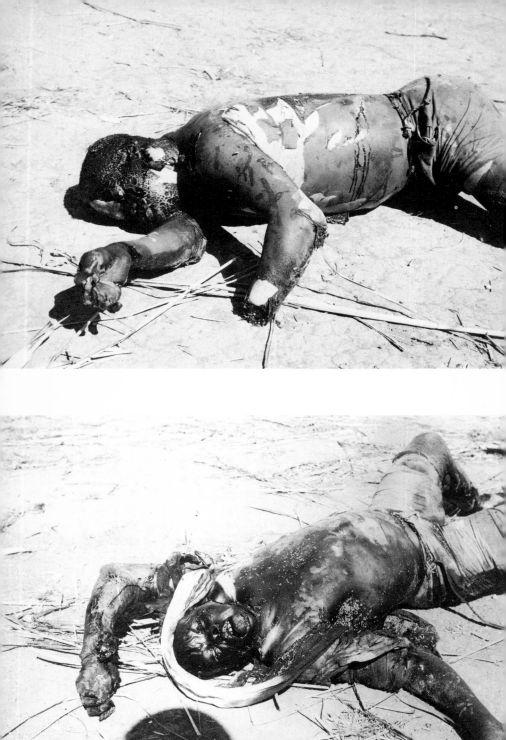

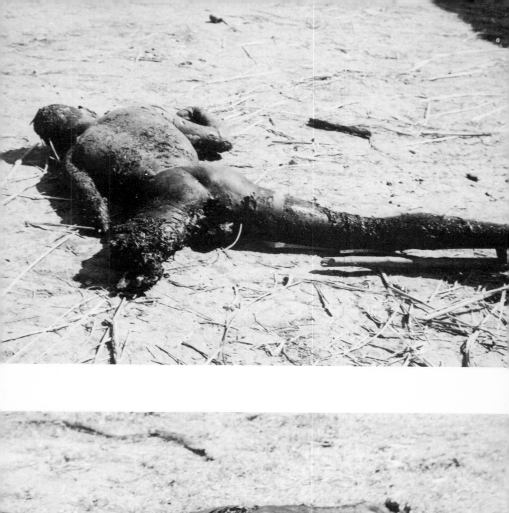

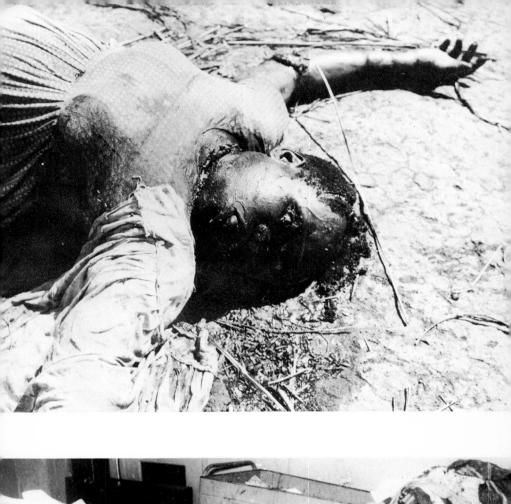

through the dirt, into the sawmill, dozens of bodies, including the two sleepy guards that had been at the border post and the watchman who had walked out to see what the commotion was in the village. As it turned out, the bleeding bodies being dragged into the sawmill were forty-two, some of them women, and a few of them boys and girls in their teens—the entire white population of Luvo. The terrorist band must have numbered between two and three hundred, some of them wearing gleaming patent leather shoes, sports jackets and neckties, others wearing khaki trousers and sport shirts; still others barefoot, in dirty shorts. But they were all laughing and shouting as they flogged, with their *catanas*, the bodies being dragged through the dirt. The better-dressed terrorists carried rifles, but the majority had only the sharp-edged *catanas*.

"What in the name of God are they bringing the bodies here for?" Zacharias heard himself ask, as he felt a shiver of horror.

"Merciful God, merciful God!" whispered Inhaca, as he crossed himself repeatedly.

They hid the best they could behind the crates on top of the pile, but they could see the entire scene through the cracks. Zacharias made a silent prayer to the good Lord that the terrorists would not spot the truck.

One of the band, obviously a worker at the sawmill, turned on the mechanical saw, and the belts and blades began to move. As Zacharias and Inhaca strained their eyes, they saw that many of the whites were still alive, moaning in pain, the blood dripping from their wounds which had been inflicted by *catana* blows on their heads, necks and chests. Some of the terrorists began to leap wildly around the mechanical saw. From where they were, Zacharias and Inhaca could not hear any words, only laughter. They were both nearly paralyzed with fright, and Zacharias felt that his fingernails were burning and buried in the still green wood of a crate.

The terrorists began to strip the clothes off the dead and off the ones still living. Then, they strapped the bodies, the dead ones and the still living ones, to the moving plank, lengthwise, as though they were logs. They pressed down the levers and the plank began to push the bodies into the buzz saw, feet first. A few piercing, dying screams reached Zacharias' ears, and he had to take a deep breath not to faint. Inhaca had covered his eyes with the palm of his hand and he was swallowing hard.

Soon it was all over, and the terrorists left the sawmill, laughing loudly and waving their arms, like drunks returning from a gay party. They left nothing behind them but pitiful bits and pieces of human flesh strewn all over the place, and the blood still warm on the mechanical plane and buzz saw. The sun was now shining directly over the horror, but Zacharias and Inhaca kept their eyes shut and their bodies motionless, hoping foolishly that the nightmare would go away

They stayed there a very long time, until there was not a single sound coming from the village. Then, they descended from the pile of crates and crawled through the grass to the first houses of the village. They found nothing but dead silence, empty houses with broken doors and windows. The people had been reduced to discarded fragments of humanity at the sawmill, and the terrorists had gone to celebrate elsewhere. But the chickens were still alive, and they were strolling closer and closer to the sawmill, their beaks smelling the dirt, attracted more and more by the odor of the dead.

Zacharias and Inhaca crawled back to the storage yard, got into the truck, and started on the road back to São Salvador. They had little choice; the alternative would be to cross the border into the Congo, but the danger there might be even greater. Zacharias was fully conscious that the terrorists might jump his truck at any moment, but his only choice was to drive on. In his dire predicament, he had one small consolation: he had enough gasoline if he were allowed to drive on, for he always carried several extra cans for emergencies. But he had no firearms, so he kept an iron bar by his side, to give himself an illusory sense of security.

"Boy, if those savages catch us, you run like hell one way, and I run like hell the other way," Zacharias said. "They may go after me and leave you alone."

"They will not leave me alone, boss," the Kimbundo said, shaking his head.

It was almost dark when they reached the vicinity of São Salvador. Zacharias and Inhaca had exhausted their supply of bread and cheese, and they were famished. They had hoped, with misgivings, to fetch some food at São Salvador. But, at this point, a native in rags jumped from the bush into their path, waving his arms.

"May God have mercy on my soul!" Zacharias cried,

THE SAWMILL AT LUVO 83

thinking that the end had come, and he switched the engine to second gear to run over the man.

"Stop, boss!" cried Inhaca, as he went for the emergency brake. "That is no Bakongo!"

Zacharias brought the truck to an abrupt stop. The native, a boy of about twenty, rushed to the cabin. His name was Ulambo, and he was a Bailundo from southern Angola. He was a worker at the huge Primavera plantation near São Salvador. The terrorists had massacred all the Europeans at the plantation in the early morning, and also many of the Bailundo workers, but Ulambo and a few others had managed to escape.

"Hop in, boy," said Zacharias to the Bailundo. "Who were the terrorists?"

"The Bakongo workers at Primavera, and others I know not. All speak Kikongo language," Ulambo said.

"Can I go through the town?" Zacharias asked, as he started down the road again.

"Boss cannot. São Salvador full of terrorists," the Bailundo said. "Ulambo know trail wide enough for wheels that take us to Madimba road past São Salvador."

The trailer was empty, so Zacharias took the chance of driving through muddy paths. He drove in the dark, with the lights off, Inhaca and Ulambo walking ahead of the vehicle to show the way. Finally they reached the dirt road on the other side of São Salvador. From there to Bembe was approximately a hundred miles and the road was in very bad shape. Still, it would be some kind of road, rather than this muddy path. And from Bembe—if they should ever make it—to Carmona, going through Songo, would be another hundred miles.

Zacharias drove very slowly, still with the lights off, hoping and praying that the engine would not heat up too much, for he had to keep it most of the time in low gear. Inhaca and Ulambo moaned and complained about hunger. Zacharias did not complain but he was as hungry as they were.

They passed cautiously through the small village of Madimba. Nothing stirred. It would be difficult to tell whether everybody was dead or asleep. Not a light, not a soul, not even a stray chicken they could grab for food. Later on, they found here and there trunks of small trees blocking the road. They removed them with their hands, but they saw no one. The hour was late and the bush was asleep. Two hours later they went through the small village of Lucunga. Again, not a light, not a soul, not even a chicken or a goat. They drove on towards Bembe.

They arrived in the vicinity of Bembe at dawn and they decided to hide the truck in a small bush by the road and cover it with tree branches. They hid there all day. Inhaca and Ulambo collected coconuts and edible fibres and a couple of tender snakes which they boiled. There was a small creek nearby and they got some water from it.

After nightfall they took off again, the lights still turned off. They had to go through Bembe. There was no other way.

"Brace yourselves, boys!" Zacharias said to his companions. "I am going to step on it."

And he drove at top speed through the large and dark village, half-blindly, praying that no logs would be blocking the road. They saw and heard nothing. Not a light, not a soul, not a noise. Way out of Bembe they came to another silent village, Tomboco, and the road became better if not good. Past Tomboco, there was an intersection well known to Zacharias, and here he had to make a decision.

The road west led to Ambrizete and the sea, but it passed through the hills of Bessa Monteiro, and if the terrorists were there, they would not have the prayer of a chance. The road southeast led to Nova Caipemba, Songo and Carmona, but it would pass by the hills of Mucaba, which would also be the end of the world for them if the terrorists were around.

"What do you say, boys?" Zacharias asked, his mind vacillating.

Ulambo, the Bailundo, was for Ambrizete and the sea. He was probably eager to find his way by freighter to southern Angola. Inhaca, the Kimbundo, was for inland and Carmona, which would bring him closer to his home grounds, Malange. Zacharias pondered briefly on the choice, but he decided for Carmona. He figured that the path inland might be safer than the coast because, with a terrorist war on, the terrorist leaders would expect people to be running toward the coast, thus, they may be cutting off the roads in that direction. As the events were subsequently known, it turned out that Zacharias' choice was a matter of life or death. Had he attempted to make the

Bessa Monteiro hills, toward the coast, he would not have lived to tell the tale.

Again they drove in the dark. But as they reached the hills of Mucaba, near Songo, they found the road absolutely impassable; dozens and dozens of big logs had been thrown across the road. They drove the truck off the road, covered it with branches, and proceeded on foot through the bush toward Songo. They took with them tools as weapons and two containers of gasoline to use as bombs, if necessary.

Daylight was breaking. They bumped here and there into groups of refugees, natives. Some of them were also trying to reach Carmona, others were making their way northward toward the Congo. They told them of the massacre at Nova Caipemba and of the killings at Songo. The ones trying to reach Carmona were running away from the terrorists, but the majority, making their way northward, said that they had heard that the Portuguese paratroopers were coming and that they would kill all the blacks. Still others were running away without any place or aim in mind. There was great confusion, but Zacharias and his two companions kept on aiming for Carmona, bypassing Songo, and eating coconuts as they found them.

That night, the evening of the seventeenth of March, Zacharias, Inhaca and Ulambo reached Carmona. On the edge of town, they were greeted by a sudden yellow spotlight and the muzzles of vigilantes' rifles.

"Who goes there?" shouted the leader of the vigilante patrol.

"Zacharias, truck driver from Ambrizete, and my helpers," Zacharias answered. "I have a story to tell—"

"Approach, with your hands up," instructed the patrol leader.

6

The Leader

"What was so special about this prisoner?" I asked the police sergeant at the Uige headquarters. He was showing me photographs of a tall Bakongo with a coarse and cruel face but, paradoxically enough, with a remarkable expression of dignity and an almost poetic fervor in his eyes.

"He claimed to be the leader of the band which attacked the M'Bridge experimental farm," the sergeant explained.

"Was he?" I asked.

"I am not sure. One is not too sure about anything these days," he said. Then he added, shrugging his shoulders, "Since he wanted to take credit for the massacre at M'Bridge, we had no choice but to believe him."

"How was he captured?" I asked. "The band got away, I understand."

"Yes," said the police sergeant, "I think he wanted to be captured, to brag about having been the leader. . . . Well, we know exactly what happened at M'Bridge from a few surviving witnesses, but we will never know for sure about this fellow. He did talk a lot, though. He talked and talked about himself, in the Kikongo language, to one of my cypaio corporals who acted as interpreter. . . . Would you like to see the cypaio's report and the testimony by one of the witnesses?"

HE HAD arrived from Leopoldville a few weeks before to organize the assault on the experimental farm at
M'Bridge. In Leopoldville he had had the honor of shaking hands with the great Holden Roberto, the leader of
the U.P.A., who in turn had shaken hands many times
with the great Lumumba and with many of the world's
great leaders in the hall of the United Nations. He felt a
communion of ideals with all those great leaders, and a
sense of brotherhood with them—a feeling which, in
turn, gave him a sense of security and destiny. He hoped
that some day in the near future he would stand side by
side with the other great leaders in the forum of the
United Nations—perhaps he might even be chosen to

address that august body. His speech, if that time should come, would be a highly moving and idealistic one, all about freedom and tyranny, and it would bring the aroused assembly to its feet. In the meantime, he would take pains to polish his French and to cultivate his accent, as Holden, his idol, had done, for he must show his future diplomatic colleagues at the United Nations that a poorly educated laborer from the wrong side of the tracks in Leopoldville is not necessarily an illiterate or a savage.

He shared many things in common with the great leader Holden Roberto. Like Holden, he too had been born in the district of São Salvador do Congo, in Portuguese Angola, a few miles from the Congo border. As in Holden's case, his family had emigrated to the Congo when he was only a child of two. But, unlike Holden, he had never had a chance for much schooling and he spoke only two or three words of Portuguese. In fact, he did not particularly hate the Portuguese. He had never had any dealings with them, and he had not returned to Angola since his departure as a child. But Holden had explained to him enthusiastically what the great cause was all about and the rewards that would come from it, and he was determined to do a good job, as good or better than any of Holden's other lieutenants. He knew that Holden would appreciate it and subsequently promote him to the top echelon of the organization.

Now he was a leader on his own, his feet planted on this strange soil of Angola from which his forefathers had come. He decided then that he would not allow himself to become an ordinary terrorist leader—he would be superior to the others, he would accomplish something that would long be remembered by the Portuguese, by the U.P.A., and by the admiring world which, Holden had told him, was on his side, the side of freedom against tyranny. These two words Holden had imprinted on his mind in a manner which he would never forget.

Perhaps some of the other assault leaders elsewhere were having identical thoughts of triumph and glory, but this possibility only increased his determination to do a superlative job on his assignment. Yet, despite his self-confidence, he was somewhat preoccupied about his friend Losso, the one in charge of the planned assault on the big Primavera plantation. Losso would try to outshine him, no doubt. Losso was very tough, knew how to hate and also had useful experiences with the Lumumba organization. Nevertheless, he was determined to outshine Losso. He was now a leader on his own.

After his great triumph at M'Bridge he learned of Losso's victory at Primavera, but from what he heard—and from the pictures which were later shown to him when he was captured—he was sure that Losso did not outshine him. It is true that Losso and his group had slaughtered with great violence all the European personnel at the vast Primavera plantation—all but a woman, a Mrs. Reis, who had been erroneously left for dead, after having been tortured and raped many times. It is true that Losso and his boys had mutilated the women in the most unforgettable way and hacked the children to pieces and hung their remains from the branches of trees. It is also true that some of the stomachs had been cut open and the insides stuffed with dry grass and bits of wood which were then set afire. Still, when he was brought over by his captors to see these things, he did not think that Losso had done better at Primavera than he had done at M'Bridge. His only mistake—a mistake Losso did not make—was to become careless afterwards and allow himself to be captured by the vengeful Portuguese.

He had no illusions about what the bloodthirsty Portuguese would do to him. He told his captors about the principles of human rights, which the United Nations upheld, rights which Holden had explained to him, and he asked that his case be brought before the United Nations, for he was a political refugee defending the cause of freedom, as Holden had explained to him. But the hateful Portuguese just stared at him, unbelievingly. Perhaps they did not understand the French language. It remained for him, before his doom, to recall proudly his triumph.

At the very early hours of dawn on the fifteenth of March, he and his group began to converge cautiously upon the M'Bridge experimental farm. On the way they passed a small farm run by an elderly European couple. They knocked down the door awakening the farmer and his wife, and the leader asked them for *aguardente* the homemade brandy, all the *aguardente* they had. The frightened farmer showed him where all his *aguardente* was, and the leader and some of his aides drank it, after which the leader told the farmer that his *aguardente* was not very good. The trembling farmer apologized but the leader would not accept his apologies. Thereupon, the leader borrowed a kitchen knife from the farmer and slit his throat with it.

He told his followers to cut off the old man's head and put it back in bed with his wife, but they must spare her, for she must be able to remember that the leader had been in her house once. After they finished the *aguardente* they left and headed for the large experimental farm.

At half-past five they were lurking in the elephant grass in the vicinity of M'Bridge which slept in deep silence. Daylight broke at six o'clock. The leader raised his machete, and shouted, *"Mata! Mata! Mata!"* Within an hour his triumph was complete.

Days later, from a hospital bed, one of the very few survivors, a subforeman named Manuel Lourenco Neves Alves, related what he saw.

" . . . At six o'clock that morning I woke up with the noise and when I came to the window of my room I saw the house of the manager of the Fazenda being attacked by hundreds of blacks, maybe four hundred of them. Most of those blacks I had never seen around M'Bridge. Almost at the same time the terrorists began to attack the other houses and installations. I grabbed my hunting rifle and started to shoot at them from my window, but I was running short of ammunition and my African houseboy, João, made a dash for the house next door to collect more ammunition. He never made it. A band of terrorists caught him, killed him with *catana* blows and then cut off his head and sexual organs. Then the crazy savages

lifted those things in the air, like trophies, and they began jumping about in a dance, yelling and whistling and laughing.

"They were bringing out the other captured men onto the ground in front of the installations and they started slaughtering them in the most horrible ways. The screaming victims were still alive when the beasts cut their eyes out of their sockets, cut their hands off, castrated them and cut their bellies open and pulled their insides out. I was trembling with horror and fear . . .

"Oh, God, what they did to my old friend, José, truly the kindest man who ever lived. The terrorists skinned him alive! The piercing screams of my old friend . . . I can still hear them in my ears!

"Then, the turn came for the women and the children. The beasts made no color discrimination. They slaughtered white, mulatto and Negro alike. They would throw the smaller children high into the air, let them drop on the soil to break their bones and then the bastards would play a brutal game of football with the bodies of those dying children, while the poor mothers screamed like crazy in the hands of the beasts. I didn't believe that anything so evil could exist in the world!

"Afterwards, they started on the women. The married women and the young girls alike. They were disrobed and raped savagely by scores of those beasts. I refuse to describe some of the horribly obscene things they did to those poor women before they finally killed them . . . the savages cut the breasts off practically each one of them and pushed sticks of wood through their lower parts as they died. Almost like cannibals, they abused the body of a pretty white girl of eighteen and then they tied her to a tree, crucified her, cut off her breasts and put one in each of her outstretched hands . . .

"I was about to use my last cartridge on myself when the terrorists jumped me and captured me alive. By this time they were fed up with blood, I guess, because they were going to give me a longer torture. They put pepper in my eyes, tied my hands and feet, and dragged me on the ground in a kind of a race.

"I guess I have to believe in miracles because I was still alive when that air force plane came flying low over the Fazenda and started machine-gunning the terrorists. they ran away like rabbits back into the forest . . ."

7

Tranquility at Mavoio

to someone I am the bud amongst the thorns
to someone I represent the ideal of the Christ child
to someone I am the life and the light in the eyes
that someone lived only to give me life
                    A. C. GONSALVES CRESPO (1846-1883)

WHAT can I tell you, sir? I had never heard of Mavoio before, and I have tried to put that memory away," the lieutenant said, as we sipped a cognac at the bar of the officers' club at the air force base of Negage. Unlike most other officers walking in and out of the club that evening, the slim lieutenant, who had made his way up from the ranks, was a member of the small military garrison in northern Angola at the time of the initial terrorist onslaught.

"It was my first war experience, so to speak," he continued thoughtfully. His infantry fatigues were worn-out and soiled, and once in a while he glanced with a touch of envy at the fur-lined leather jackets of three air force pilots sitting at a table nearby.

"Believe it or not, it was my first war experience, after so many years overseas," he went on, "but I found no one to fight and no one to rescue. Since then, I have seen a lot, and have had a few narrow escapes. Take, for instance, that morning last May when I awakened in the forest under the branches of a mango tree to stare into the eyes of a laughing Bakongo, and as I jerked my body aside, trying to avoid the blow from his *catana*, my elbow accidentally hit the trigger of my submachine gun, and my hair was singed but the terrorist got it all on his face. . . .

". . . Oh, yes, but you want to hear about Mavoio, sir. On the morning of that day, I mean, of course, the fifteenth of March; first there were the rumors, then reports from here and there. All around us, practically. In the afternoon the captain called me into his office and said, 'Lieutenant, you take a patrol and set out for Mavoio. We hear that a band of terrorists is headed for that village,' and I asked him, 'Where is Mavoio?' He gave me a section of a map he had on his desk, which showed a tiny speck about a dozen kilometers from Quibocolo on the road between Damba and Maquela do Zombo. According to the map there was some sort of dirt road connecting Quibocolo with Mavoio. In short, about forty miles from the Congo border. The captain recommended, 'Travel by foot and avoid the road. You should make it by morning.' He allowed me two dozen soldiers, half of them Africans, including an Army photographer and two medics. Off we went, mostly through the elephant grass and patches of jungle, never too far from the main path which the map said was a road.

"Practically nobody said a word until the early morning when we reached a high ground overlooking a small valley where we saw a few farm houses. We had slept about an hour, but it was so sticky and the *cassimbo* was so cold that we preferred to walk. We saw a few snakes here and there but we did not touch them. We saw no human being, friend or foe . . . This round on me, sir. Thank you.

"There we stood on the crest of the little hill, our heads slightly above the *capim*, watching. It all looked very peaceful and tranquil. 'It looks as though the terrorists missed this one,' the patrol sergeant whispered in my ear. And I said, 'It looks that way. Why are you whispering, man?' We walked about half a mile farther, still inside the *capim*, and then the sergeant pointed his finger at a small cluster of white houses down below. 'That must be the village,' he said. We approached it cautiously. Nothing stirred. 'All right, sergeant,' I said. 'You stay here with the others and I'll go in myself. One long whistle means I fell into a trap and three short ones mean all clear.'

"So I walked into the village taking along two of my Bailundo soldiers who can smell Bakongo traps better than anybody else. There was a slight wind and the unlocked doors and windows were kind of dancing in the breeze, but otherwise the tranquility was complete. Even the gardens and orchards in front of the little white houses were spotless. I stood there in the middle of the road, staring at the swinging doors in the wind; Mavoio was deserted. 'The villagers must have fled in a hurry! I wonder where they went,' I said to my Bailundo corporal.

He was sniffing the air. 'There is a bad smell, lieutenant,' the corporal said.

"Then I saw the dead cat right in front of the doorway of the first house. A calico cat, black, white and yellow, cut in half by the blow of a *catana*. We cocked our submachine guns and went into that first house. Everything was smashed inside. In the bedroom we found a broken alarm clock on the floor. It had stopped at six-forty, and from what we saw later we figured that the terrorists had come through Mavoio the previous morning. In that house there were no children. Just a couple, relatively young. They were both in bed. The man had his insides out on the sheet. They had cut him lengthwise, from the chin down. The body of the woman was a horror to look at. They had cut off her breasts and driven the blades of their *catanas* through her eyes, among other things. I took a strong gulp of brandy from my canteen and came out to look into the next house. More or less the same thing, except that this other couple and two of their African servants had been slaughtered in their living room. 'They are long gone, lieutenant,' the corporal said. He meant, of course, the killers. I gave three short whistles and the rest of the patrol entered the village with the usual precautions.

"It was a small village but not one single living thing, man, woman, child, dog or cat was left. And somehow the slaughter, the atrocities and the blood were all indoors. Outdoors, the village was the neatest I have seen. That is, until we came to the last white house which had a stone patio in the back. That particular family must have been out early in the morning. We found them all on the patio behind the house: the mother, the father, and three children, one of them still in the crib. They had even cut off the arms and legs of the little baby in the crib. That's when I rushed behind a tree in the backyard to vomit. My Bailundo corporal was also rushing but he did not make the tree. Funny thing, sir, the only thought occurring to me then was that this was the first time I had seen one of my African soldiers vomit from anything other than too much *aguardente*.

"The Army photographer was busy taking pictures all over the place and the medics began to collect the remains of the people and the other soldiers began to dig temporary graves for them. There was a handful of African servants who had shared the fate of their masters. Nobody said much, as we went about the grim business of collecting the remains and burying them. No one in my patrol touched his rations that day but we exhausted our supply of brandy and *aguardente*. I made a short prayer over the graves, everybody knelt in silence, and that was the end of Mavoio.

"Just before sunset the patrol made a reconnaissance of the valley but we found no traces of terrorists, and in the evening we started back to our base where we arrived in the morning of the 17th. After the plates were developed the sergeant asked for a print of that picture of the baby in the crib. He carries it in his wallet and always takes it with him whenever he goes in the bush looking for Bakongo terrorists."

8

A Prayer for Madimba

. . . was it to see these horrors,
oh my child,
that mother nursed you to her breasts,
that God gave you such pretty eyes?
oh my child,
you had better be blind . . .
ANTONIO NOBRE (1867-1900)

"WHEN you think of it from the distance of a year
—past the initial shock—you almost feel that each incident was more horrible than the other," said the polished
agronomist at São Salvador, as we strolled along the main
street of town, that is, the unpaved road which runs north
to the Congo border at Luvo, "the sawmill village," about
forty miles away.

The evening was cool, a hesitant moon greeted us
through the misty *cassimbo* which was beginning to
gather overhead. I heard laughter coming from a tavern
nearby, but I saw no tropical flowers sprouting from the
vines caressing my hair as I passed, and the reminis-
cences of the senseless savagery which had befallen many
places around São Salvador was everpresent in my mind.

"Incredible is a word we often use," the agronomist
continued. "It can mean everything or nothing. But here
it truly meant incredible . . . I mean, what happened at
Madimba. It's something that even I refuse to believe, al-

though I went there to see the picture with my own eyes.

"Madimba is not too far from here, some forty-three kilometers on the road southeast to Lucunga and Bembe. It was a rather prosperous agricultural center where the relations between the white farmers and storekeepers, on one side, and the Bakongos, on the other, appeared to be excellent. So much so that none of these farmers and storekeepers actually kept firearms. In a sense, that was the beginning of the great tragedy which struck them on March 16, one day after the great Terror Day. But perhaps I should let you speak to one of the Madimba men who lives now here at São Salvador."

"But I thought that everyone—" I began.

"No, no," my informant interrupted, "not a single one of the men of Madimba was killed or hurt, and this somehow makes the story of Madimba even more tragic. Here is the house. He must be in because the lights are on. People here save their electricity when they are out."

A patrol jeep drove by very slowly and the soldiers in it, wearing the habitual camouflage uniform, waved at us. A hundred yards away I saw a fence of barbed wire and near it a yellow floodlight passed regularly over the edges of the trees and the *capim*. The agronomist knocked at the door and a robust man in his late thirties, with all appearances of a peasant farmer, came to the door.

After the brief introductions the agronomist said to the farmer, "José, I want you to come for a stroll with us. My friend here would like to ask you something." Without a word of pleasure or protest the man went back into the house, fetched his woolen coat and joined us on the street. The evening was quite cool and the low *cassimbo* was beginning to spread its fingers of mist through the barbed wire.

"The gentleman would like to hear about Madimba ... in your own words, José," the agronomist said, as we resumed our walk.

"Why does the gentleman want to hear about that?" the man asked, as he lit a black cigarette.

"I saw some pictures ..." I told him.

"That's more than I care to look at. I saw it with my own eyes and that's enough for a lifetime," the farmer said.

"Go on, Jose," the agronomist urged him.

"You see, sir, we are very stupid, the men of Madimba," the farmer began. "We sit right here in our new houses in the village and we only think of our crops and our card game in the evening. A few laughs when we get together, and a couple of bottles of wine, too. We get along well with the Bakongos in Madimba, we laugh with them and sometimes we even drink with them. Now, sir, we are not far from the Congo and we know of many things happening over there. But we say to ourselves, 'It cannot happen here.' We are stupid and wrong because that day of March 15 we hear that the Congolese blacks, some of them Bakongos from around here, some of them Bakongos from the Congo side, are killing our people right and left. We hear terrible things happening at Primavera, M'Bridge and other places, and we feel in a kind of panic.

"Now, sir, we, the men, are very stupid at Madimba.

Nobody has firearms, except for two old hunting rifles that don't fire, anyhow. Oh, Lord, what can we do? We get together, just the white people of Madimba, and some of the blacks we trust as our friends, and we think that the only thing to do is to run to the town of São Salvador, right here, for arms and help, a good eight leagues by the road. This is in the early morning of March 16. But what to do with the women and children? We cannot leave them in the village at the mercy of the savages, if they come, and we cannot drag them along through the bush to São Salvador. We dare not use the road.

"So, we find a safe spot for them in a thick wood a few kilometers from the village, away from any paths and bush trails. We leave water and food with them, and all the women keep their rosaries in order to pray while we go for help."

The farmer paused for a long time as we turned around to make our way back to his house.

"We are so stupid leaving the women and children alone like that," he continued, "but we think the hidden place in the wood is safe. A few of us should stay with the women. It happens just the same, if some of us stay, but then the women are not alone. We arrive here in São Salvador and we get some firearms and a few other people come along to help us, including the engineer here. Then we find our way back to the spot in the wood near Madimba where we left our women and children. . . . Some of the men cannot even look at what's left of them. But I look and look and look and I cannot believe my eyes. Three of the men who looked at it like I did, they just went out of their minds and started beating their heads against the trunks of trees. I guess I am luckier than most: I had only a wife there, I had no children . . . Good night, engineer . . . Good night, sir."

And the farmer turned his back on us abruptly and went into his house.

"No one will ever know exactly how the terrorists found that almost impenetrable spot where the women and children were hiding," the agronomist said, as we resumed our walk. "But we can surmise more or less what happened from what we saw. The terrorists went into Madimba which they found deserted. They proceeded to destroy everything in sight. But they were bloodthirsty, so after the destruction of the village they proceeded to beat the *capim* and the woods, yelling, 'Mata, UPA! Mata, UPA!' and other cries to intimidate the hidden fugitives. Perhaps the frightened children began to cry and this would have given away their hiding place. . . .

"What those beasts did to the helpless women and children of Madimba defies any description. It was even worse, I think, than the horrible atrocities of Luvo, M'Bridge and other places. They disrobed all the women and children, and after raping the women savagely they committed on their dead bodies the most obscene butchery and mutilation. I will spare you the details, my friend . . . one lacks words to picture the horror. Besides, you saw some of the photographs we took at the time. Of all that pitiful pile of humanity, one image has stuck like glue in my memory. . . . It was the cut-off arm of a woman, the hand still desperately clutching her rosary."

9

The Photographs

... and the Vision whispers in my dream:
I have come from afar in search of your heart
to bring it peace and relief, my sleeping friend,
but I stare at her in painful surprise
(the night is arid as my own infinite.)
I stare at her with darkened, glassy eyes
and I reply: forgive me, benevolent Death,
for I have already died and died . . .

ANTHERO DE QUENTAL (1842-1891)

"THIS is the place," my companion, the photographer from Luanda, said, as he pointed to the burned-up buildings ahead of us. Our Land Rover proceeded slowly, following the zigzagging path of the military jeep ahead of us, the driver of which was trying to avoid, by instinct, any land mines buried in the dusty, narrow road. We were coming to a large commercial plantation, called "Maria José," which is located about thirty kilometers west of Negage, the chief Portuguese air force base in northern Angola.

Minutes later as we alighted from our vehicles a vast spectacle of desolation and ruin greeted my eyes. All the buildings—offices, sleeping quarters, dining hall, school, hospital, chapel and warehouses—had been burned to a crisp, and now, several months after the fire, the Maria José plantation was still abandoned to its fate, surrounded by a hostile jungle, the tall *capim* grass and stretching wild weeds taking over the management of the once rich plantation.

"Two Army photographers and I arrived here on the fourth of June," the photographer explained as we walked slowly around the burned ghosts of the buildings, "that is, three days after the slaughter. The massacre here took place in the early hours of June 1, two and a half months after the big killings further north. Not a single white person was at the plantation on the night the terrorists struck. The few European employees were absent on business."

"What is this?" I asked, as we came to the burned chapel and I saw the small and slightly burned wooden statue of the Virgin Mary resting on a plumed velvet hat which had been laid on a flat grave of earth.

"A kind of humane touch by one of the terrorists . . . the only humane touch about this ghastly business," the photographer explained. "Apparently, one of the terrorists must have been a friend of the fellow buried there, because he took the trouble to bury him, placing the victim's favorite hat over the grave, and salvaging a Virgin Mary from the burning chapel to give added comfort to the dead one. All the other victims were left at the spots where they were killed and mutilated. The name of the fellow under the earth there was Quiluange Uola, of the Cuale people. He did treasure his plumed velvet hat and he was also a Catholic, as were more than half of the workers here, judging from the rosaries and images of saints we found in the debris."

As we turned around to take a look inside of what had been the sleeping quarters for bachelor workers, a band of black birds flew away in a clatter from a dark corner of the building and an enormous rat, in panic, dashed past the photographer's legs into the bright sun outside.

"You see that burned beam there?" the photographer asked, pointing to what was left of the ceiling. "A fellow was hanging from that beam, completely naked. He obviously had been caught by several shots as he tried to escape through the high ceiling. The expression of fright on his face, with his teeth buried in the wood of the beam, and his big eyes practically leaping out of their sockets—that's something I will never forget. His body was hanging from the beam in the most grotesque fashion. It looked as though it was actually suspended by its genital organs! Imagine, being in that horrible posture for three days, and dead! I took several pictures of him."

I walked out of the dormitory to catch my breath. Presently I sat down on a rock by the *capim* grass, contemplating the scene, and I pulled out of my pocket the "Maria José Memo," copy of which a friend of mine had obtained for me in Luanda. It was a somewhat ceremonious report addressed to the governor general and written by a conscientious Luanda bureaucrat who had accompanied the three photographers to the Maria José plantation. It read:*

* literal translation

"His Excellency
The Governor General of Angola
Palace of the Government
Luanda, Angola

Luanda, June 10, 1961

"Excellency:

"I have the great honor to bring to Your Excellency's attention the result of the mission with which I was entrusted, and which, I earnestly hope, has been carried out in a manner to justify the trust Your Excellency has kindly bestowed upon my humble person.

"As a result of Your Excellency's directive, I proceeded on June 2 with three photographers to the town of Negage, situated twenty-odd kilometers from the site of the Maria José plantation. Upon our arrival at Negage I solicited from the local commandant the support of a military detachment to accompany us to the above mentioned plantation. On the strength of Your Excellency's letter of recommendation, the commandant graciously placed at our disposal a small motorized escort, under the command of a gallant officer of the Dragoons, Lieutenant of Cavalry J. A. Bruno.

"The dirt road from Negage to the site of the Maria José plantation was most uncomfortable and hazardous, and quite dangerous, I may add, due to the tall *capim* grass and thick forest flanking our way on both sides. With the utmost alertness we proceeded on, cautiously, and thus we arrived without incident at a point less than five kilometers from the plantation. Here, the first vehicle fell into a trap—a huge hole in the road cleverly covered with canvas and dust. Curiously enough, the trap was almost exactly the size of the vehicle which fell into it, thus rendering it impossible for the three men inside to escape immediately, as the vehicle in reference had a hard top! We realized instantly that we had fallen into an ambush, and this realization was as instantly confirmed by volleys of gunfire from the *capim* on both sides of the road. Perhaps we would not have been able to obtain the photographs, which I have the honor to remit to Your Excellency herewith, were it not for the swift and capable reaction of our escort leader, Lieutenant Bruno.

"Within a few brief seconds the lieutenant and his soldiers were counterattacking the hidden terrorists, using for that purpose the machine gun mounted on one of the jeeps, as well as hand grenades and bazookas. Fortunately, the casualties on our side were negligible, due principally to the poor aim of the attackers: a corporal lost two fingers, a soldier had his stomach torn off by enemy fire, and another soldier found a bullet in his knee cap. After the barrage of machine gun and bazooka fire, and the tossing of hand grenades, our gallant lieutenant, revolver in hand, and his soldiers charged upon the hidden enemy position where they found four dead terrorists and a few others who were too wounded to be carried away. The remainder of the attackers vanished into the bush, as usual.

"Due to the state of our wounded, we began to retreat toward the village of Dimuca, but before we reached that destination, we had to remove the huge trunk of a tree blocking the road. Again we were attacked by the enemy in the bush; their numbers appeared to have increased, judging from the amount of fire directed against our vehicles and men. Lieutenant Bruno once again reacted swiftly and competently, but we were not making any headway, despite the insignificance of our casualties. Happily, at this juncture, fighter planes from the Negage air base appeared overhead and began low strafing of the terrorist band. The bandits vanished again. (On our eventual return to Negage we learned from the two pilots who came to our rescue that, had we reached the village of Dimuca, we might have come to a sad end, for the terrorists and their sympathizers had congregated in that village in a gigantic ambush, waiting for us.)

"After this second attack was frustrated, we turned back toward the Maria José plantation which we finally reached without further incidents, although the wounded were feeling most uncomfortable. On our way back to the Maria José we rescued the three men still trapped in their vehicle. For that purpose we had to lift half of the vehicle from the hole in the ground. The reason why these patient three men were not rescued before was that in the heat of the first battle we had forgotten about them and they were, apparently, too polite to shout for help.

"Excellency:

"After all these ordeals we finally arrived at the Maria José plantation. The grim spectacle we found is conveyed, at least in part, by the collection of glossy prints submitted herewith.

"According to the investigation carried out by the military patrol, and from the interrogation *in loco* of the two surviving witnesses (two native workers who managed to hide in the grass from whence they were able to see without being seen), the plantation was assaulted in the very early hours of the first of June by a large band of terrorists belonging to a sect of this region which has connections with terrorist groups operating from the Congo. This sect is known as the 'tocoistas.' There were fifty-two workers, some of them with families, at the plantation at the time of the assault. Most of them were voluntary workers from the Cuale people, a few from the Negage area, and fewer even were Bailundos from the south. Still, a number of them were 'tocoistas,' and these, of course, made common cause with the terrorists, helping in the slaughter of their fellow workers.

"According to the testimony of the two witnesses—*a*) João Continuo, a Bailundo, 20 years of age, native of Candande; *b*) Jurga, of the Cuale people, age undetermined—approximately one hundred terrorists entered the plantation unexpectedly before the break of dawn and were promptly joined by about a dozen workers and their families who must have been allied to the band. Thereupon the terrorists began the mass killing with great dispatch, using mostly the traditionally long and sharp *catanas*, although many of the attackers also had firearms, especially *canhangulos*. The operation of the massacre was conducted by a former foreman of the Maria José, known as Corporal Ramos.

"The majority of the victims were asleep when the assault took place. On inspecting the photographs herewith, Your Excellency will verify that many of the victims are lying on their beds or else by the side of their beds. Others attempted to escape from their rooms or dormitory and were cut down in the act, for their bodies hung from windows or lay on the threshold of doors. Some others succeeded in reaching the central patio only to meet the same dreadful fate there. Your Excellency will verify, from the enlarged photographs, that most of the victims were slain and mutilated with *catanas*, though others were first shot with *canhangulos*, and many others were burned with gasoline (the supply of which was abundant at the plantation,) judging from the terrifying appearance of their bodies. In most cases, the terrorists dedicated themselves to the gruesome task of cutting up the limbs and heads of the victims. Among the bodies we found two women, one of them in a state of pregnancy, as well as a very young boy and two children.

"Excellency:

"The spectacle which we saw, and which I have attempted to describe succinctly to Your Excellency, reveals the most evil fury and cannibalistic instincts on the part of the contemptible terrorists!

"As I do not wish to burden Your Excellency with too many details of this pitiful tragedy, I shall omit many other terrible aspects of my mission. Immediately upon our arrival and inspection, the lieutenant ordered his soldiers to prepare a huge burial ditch. The corpses were so decomposed and so replete with vermin, vermin which by now was also covering the patio and floors of the buildings, that it became necessary to proceed with a burial en masse at once. (After hundreds of photographs were taken of course.) During the burial many of the soldiers became ill with nausea and vomited, due principally to the asphyxiating odor, and had to be excused temporarily from their duty. After the sad task was completed, it became necessary to cover the grounds with gasoline and set fire to it, in order to destroy the vermin, lest public health be effected.

"As Your Excellency will verify from the photographs taken during the mass burial, the tragic scene is reminiscent of some of the most horrible scenes prevalent in certain concentration camps during the last world war, but the spirit with which we carried out our grim task was a much different one. We regretted our inability to give individual burial to each one of the badly decomposed cadavers, but we did place a wooden cross over the mass graveyard, prayers were said by the lieutenant and followed by us and, as a finale, a platoon of soldiers in impeccable formation gave a military farewell to the victims and fired several volleys into the air.

"After which, Excellency, we proceeded to our vehicles for the dangerous return trip to Negage.

"From the records we were able to find in the office of the plantation, from the testimony of the two eyewitnesses, the native workers Continuo and Jurga, and from the reports of the two European employees, Barraqueiro and Calixto, who were not at the plantation at the time of the massacre, we presume that, among the forty bodies we buried, there were the following thirty-six people:

Mauricio

Andre Pinto

Jose Bento

Manuel Bumba

Eugenio Cacala

Maria Bento

Maria Bumba

João (a child)

OF THE CUALE PEOPLE

Bernardo Quiluange

Queta Quiluange (a child)

Quiluange Uola

Ferraz Gonga

Jacinto Massango

Agostinho Bravo

Armando Zua

Fonseca Vunge

Albino Dala

Tomaz Camuege

Mario Catenda

Samuel Lenga

Ferraz Camuege

Jose Cabaca

Cassua Quissanga

Faustino

Manuel Capemba

Daniel Cabaca

Luamba Gunza

Joaquim Ebo

João Curiba

Joaquim Quisanga

Neves Gonga

Albino Zua

Bernardo (a child)

FROM DIMUCA

Quimbuari Luma (foreman)   Malau Cambige

Mulaza Mahula (foreman)

"Excellency:

"It was not possible to obtain even tentative identification of four of the bodies, due to the insufficiency of the records and the extremely advanced stage of decomposition of the corpses. Even amongst the names of the victims listed above, there is the distinct possibility of an error or two, that is to say that I may have listed as dead two or three Cuale workers who may have joined the terrorists, in which case the respective bodies would belong, of course, to two or three others whom we listed as having gone with the terrorists. As I had previously pointed out to Your Excellency, on the excellent corroboration of the eyewitnesses, Continuo and Jurga, about a dozen workers—not a single one of them Bailundo, of course—made common cause with the terrorists.

"Therefore, Your Excellency, the two packages of photographs, labelled *A* and *B*, appertain entirely to scenes and deceased persons we found at this unfortunate Maria José plantation.

"The third package of photographs, labelled *C*, refers to another and smaller massacre, yet of exceedingly savage proportions, which took place near Camabatela at the plantation owned by the German national, Herr Karl Hucking.

"As the signatory of these lines was not present at that other location when our photographers took the pictures herewith, it remains for me to convey to Your Excellency some of the pertinent details which were verified by our photographers *in loco*, and which emphasize the particular fiendishness of these crimes, faithfully captured by the cameras of our photographers. For example, the pregnant native woman appearing in several of the enclosed glossy prints was bearing the child of one of the German nationals on the plantation, specifically, the son of the proprietor, according to common knowledge at Camabatela.

"The other three *mestizo* children of the same woman,

also fathered by the same white man, were savagely slain, cut up and burned by the crazed terrorists who, not satisfied with so horrible a deed, tossed the pitiful remains of the children into the buckets where the hogs were fed, the hogs being the only living things which escaped the massacre at the Hucking plantation.

"Excellency:

"The lines above are a succinct resume of the tragic events documented by the photographs contained in the three packages, labelled A, B and C. The slight delay in forwarding these photographs to Your Excellency's office was due to a clerical error for which I am partly responsible, since it occurred in my own office: without carefully examining the character of the pictures in question, one of my subaltern clerks shipped them off to the Department of Tourism. Presently, the error was discovered and corrected.

"I avail myself of this opportunity to present to Your Excellency the assurances of my highest consideration."

10

The Execution

The first time I met Thiago—the dashing but somewhat sardonic paratroop sergeant who had bright blue eyes, streaks of yellow hair, and a square long jaw—he and I were in Angola, riding in a jeep driven with insane recklessness by the chaplain of Thiago's battalion. Both the sergeant and I were livid with fright. In that particular instance I was accompanying them on a leisurely social mission to the barracks of another paratroop company and engaged in nothing more dangerous than the distribution of cigarette and chocolate gifts to the young soldiers.

"The priest thinks he is immune to road accidents because of his special deal with God," Thiago complained bitterly to me after we arrived trembling at our destination. "But someday he's going to learn that not even God himself can go on forever making sharp turns at that speed on these narrow roads. I am supposed to be his driver and nursemaid, but in the meantime he is driving me crazy."

"Can't you ask for another assignment?" I asked him.

"I could, sir, but this is the most dangerous assignment of the entire battalion and nobody else wants it," he replied, half-seriously.

A few weeks later I met Thiago again, this time in the air. He looked quite relaxed and pleased with himself.

"The poor chaplain broke his right arm badly in a jump last week," Thiago told me, trying to sound sympathetic. "So, his jeep driving is off indefinitely!"

It was during that flight that I asked him how he felt about the peculiar silent war in which he was involved.

"WELL, sir, a man reacts to these situations from his own feelings and experiences," the young paratroop sergeant said thoughtfully as he fondled the green ribbon hanging from his green beret. I was flying with him in an old Skymaster transport over the terrorist-infested region of Nuambuangongo.

"Some soldiers do not talk or even think about the things they have experienced here," he continued. "I like to talk about them. But if I should go back home to Lisbon and tell my relatives about some of the horrors I have seen, they would think I was talking for effect. I see that the newspapers in Lisbon describe this peculiar war up here as a routine mopping-up operation, with no details. That is why a man ought to get callous and pretend that it is all routine. Take my first war experience here, for instance. It was so sickening that my stomach will now take almost anything.

"It was about a week after my own company had been flown up here from Portugal. We had a report that an isolated plantation near Bembe, which is about a half-hour flying time northwest of Carmona, was under attack by a band of terrorists. My own platoon was dispatched in an old DC-3. We spotted the plantation and we were dropped on a clearing not too far from it. We made our way through the bush to the plantation but when we reached it, everything was finished. The houses, the stores and the crops had been burned to a crisp. The eleven white people on the plantation, including two women and four children, had been mutilated and abused beyond anything you can imagine, sir. We had heard of the horrible atrocities of the terrorists at the Primavera plantation, at Buela, at M'Bridge, at Nova Caipemba, at Quitexe, at Luvo, and elsewhere, but we had never seen it. When we faced those incredible sights —of arms, legs, heads strewn all over the patio of the main house—some of the boys, including myself, just threw up. The lieutenant did not, but his face was green and his hands were shaking. All he could say was, 'I want to find those animals and cut them to pieces if it is the last thing I do,' which, of course, is not the proper thing for an officer in charge of an operation to say, but all of us felt exactly the same way. Six of the Bailundo workers had also been slain, but their mutilation was minor by comparison.

"As we stared at the horrible sight, two of the Bailundo workers came down from the foliage of a tree which somehow had survived the fire. They told us that the terrorists could not have gone very far and they pointed out the direction they had taken. We took the two Bailundos along and found the trail at once. It was easy to follow because they had broken branches right and left as they fled. After more than an hour's chase we felt that we were getting very close to them.

"Suddenly we came to a small *sanzala* in the wood, and everything was peaceful, and there were no more broken branches. A group of Muchicongos, which is a branch of the Bakongo tribe, were sitting on the ground, singing a kind of *landum,* one of them beating a low drum, some of them hanging on to their pipes and all of them looking sleepy and peaceful. 'There they are!' cried the two Bailundos, and the boys were about to let go with their submachine guns, but the lieutenant told them to wait until we were absolutely sure. The ground was fresh in one spot and we found the *catanas,* still bloody, buried there, and also a few *canhangulos,* which is a Bakongo homemade scatter gun.

"The lieutenant ordered us to tie up the terrorists and take them back to the plantation. The hands and shirts of many were still bloody. Among them was a boy of twelve or thirteen. He, too, had blood on his hands, and the Bailundos said that the boy had entertained himself carving up one of the children at the plantation. When

we returned to the scene the lieutenant made the terrorists dig up the graves and collect the remains of the murdered people and bury them. Then the lieutenant said a prayer over their graves. After that, he made the terrorists dig their own graves a distance away from the others. Then, he selected a firing squad to execute the murderers. I was put in charge of that squad.

"We lined them up against the burned side of the house, their hands tied and their faces against the wall. As we were about to fire, the twelve-year-old boy with the bloody hands turned around to stare at us, as though the whole thing were a game. I yelled, 'Fire!' to my squad, the guns blazed away and they all fell, except the boy. Funny thing! We were all supposed to be crack shots but everyone missed the little monster.

"I stepped forward, drew my revolver to finish the job but the little terrorist kept on staring at me and I could not pull the trigger. I lowered the revolver and looked up at the lieutenant. The lieutenant frowned, stepped forward, pointed his revolver at the head of the boy, and we waited. We waited and waited. Finally, there was a shot and the boy fell, but the shot had not come from the lieutenant's revolver. We looked around and we saw an unshaven white man in rags, holding a rifle in his hands. Nobody said a word, and the man turned around quietly and disappeared in the bush. We learned later that this man used to live in a small farm not far from the plantation. On March 15 his entire family had been slain by terrorists while he was away. When he came home and found them dead and mutilated he took to the bush with his rifle."

The Avenger

. . . with great blows I knock at the door and cry:
I am the vagabond, the driftless one
open up, golden doors, to heal my soul!
the golden doors open with a clatter
but inside I only find, oh my despair,
silence and darkness and no more . . .
ANTHERO DE QUENTAL

ALTHOUGH Malange is situated on a high plateau in the northeast of Angola, normally enjoying a pleasant climate, it was unbearably hot at noon of the day I landed there, on my way to the interior. The air force captain, who had given me a courtesy airplane ride from Luanda, suggested that we try to get a drink before we proceeded to the hotel dining room for a meal.

We entered the town's newest cafe, a small but gleaming room with glass tables and an attractive bar. Two customers were sitting pensively at the bar, two others playing dominoes while an idle one smoked in silence and observed the game. We took the table next to the domino players. The captain snapped his fingers and the barman who was watching the two contemplative customers at the bar raised his eyelids and seemed to notice us.

"Gin and tonic!" the captain shouted across the room.

The two men at the bar turned their necks slowly but their gaze appeared to travel above our heads. The barman made a painful motion to reach for the bottle of gin.

"It is very hot today and we do not have airconditioning yet," the barman said, as he brought us the drinks.

"Oh, yes," remarked the domino watcher, without raising his eyes from the game.

We were sipping our drinks in silence when a new customer entered the cafe. This one was a big, barrel-chested man of about forty, his clothes soiled and unpressed, his face unshaven. The most noticeable thing about him was the stony, almost dead, look in his eyes.

The watcher of the domino game raised his eyes from the game, waved his hand and said to the newcomer, "*Viva*, Ze Marques!"

The newcomer halted briefly, turned his head slowly to the greeter, waved his hand in return and proceeded to the bar. Without sitting down he snapped his fingers and ordered, in a throaty voice, "*Aguardente.*" The barman took his eyes away from his two pensive customers, made a grimace, poured the alcohol from a bottle into a small glass which he pushed reluctantly toward the unkempt customer who raised the glass to his mouth with his left hand, while his right hand searced in his pocket, unsuccessfully, for the coins to pay for the drink. He drank the *aguardente* in two long, slow gulps, after which he wiped his mustache on the dirty sleeve of his coat and stared blankly at the outstretched hand of the barman.

"No money?" the barman asked, in disgust.

"No money," the peculiar customer replied, stonily.

The barman shrugged his shoulders and snapped his fingers, in a gesture of both irritation and resignation.

"I will pay for his drink," the captain said. The barman shrugged his shoulders again.

The penniless, unshaven customer turned around and started for the door. The domino watcher raised his head again from the game, waved his hand and said, "Goodbye, Ze Marques!" but the man only waved his hand in return and disappeared through the door.

"Poor Ze Marques!" exclaimed the domino watcher.

"Why?" asked one of the domino players, his voice revealing little interest in the matter.

"Seventeen," said the other domino player. "That puts me up."

"You are too lucky," said the first domino player.

"Because of what happened to him," said the domino watcher.

"What happened to whom?" asked the player.

"To Ze Marques. Did you never hear of Ze Marques?" asked the watcher.

"No. Did you?" asked the player.

"That was what I was telling you about . . . about Ze Marques," said the watcher.

"What is the matter with everybody!" exclaimed the captain, "I guess it must be the heat."

"I did not know you were telling me about Ze Marques. I do not know him, anyway," said the first domino player.

"Ze Marques and his wife used to have a small food store at Ritondo," the watcher said.

"That is right," said one of the melancholy customers

at the bar, as though he had just arrived from a long trip. "Ritondo is only a few kilometers north of here."

"Do you know Ze Marques?" asked the domino watcher.

"No, but I have been to Ritondo," said the bar customer. He promptly lost interest in the conversation and sank back into his pensive mood.

"Two more gins and tonic!" shouted the captain, as he wiped the perspiration from his forehead.

"Ze Marques came to town to buy some supplies, that day in March," the watcher said. "When he returned to Ritondo he saw three blacks running out of his store."

"Nine!" cried the second player, triumphantly.

"You are too lucky," complained the first player.

Noticing that only the captain and myself were listening to him, the domino watcher moved over to a position between the domino table and ours, and the rest of his monologue was addressed to us.

"Ze Marques recognized one of these blacks running out of his store," the man continued. "He did not know his name or where he came from, but he had seen him around many times. Ze Marques rushed into his store and found his poor wife in a pool of blood, dying. The savages had pushed their *catana* knives right through the poor lady's lower parts. Ze Marques almost lost his mind. Since that day he has lived for only one thing: to find that one killer he recognized. Ze Marques could not find him in Ritondo, so he came down here to Malange, and every morning he came to the railway station and remained there all day waiting. I saw all this because I work at the station. I am a dispatcher. 'Sooner or later he will come through here, they all do,' Ze Marques told me. Ze Marques never changed. He just stood there, day after day, waiting quietly. One afternoon last September, I was talking to him when he saw his man walking along the tracks toward the platform. 'There he is. Excuse me,' Ze Marques said to me, and he stepped toward the creature. When the creature saw Ze Marques, he tried to run away, but Ze Marques is a powerful man and he grabbed the killer's neck quickly. Then Ze Marques knocked him down and beat his head against the rail with such strength and fury that soon the creature's brains were strewn on the tracks. Ze Marques never went back to Ritondo or to the railway station, but I see him once in a while coming into a cafe for a spot of *aguardente*. . . ."

Afterword: The Context of the Angolan Revolt

BY JAMES BURNHAM

ANGOLA covers half a million square miles on the west coast of Africa, equal in area to France, Germany, Spain and Portugal combined. Its coastline stretches for a thousand miles from the mouth of the Congo River, six degrees south of the Equator, to the mouth of the Kunene at seventeen degrees south. Landward, it borders the former Belgian Congo for thirteen hundred miles on the north and northwest; then Northern Rhodesia (Zambia) on the west, and Southwest Africa on the south. For the most part, Angola lies within the zone of what geographers call "savannah" climate, with a region of drier "warm steppes" climate in the south. The terrain consists of a coastal plain eighty to one hundred miles wide, which rises in a series of terraces to the great African plateau that in the Angolan sector has an altitude of from three to five thousand feet. The climate of much of the plateau region is moderate, with adequate rainfall, well suited to both agriculture and stock raising.

There are several ports: principally Luanda, the chief city, with a quarter of a million inhabitants, and Lobito, the terminal of the Benguella railroad which extends to the Katanga copper mines. The principal agricultural products include sugar, coffee, corn, palm oil and timber, all of which are exported as well as consumed locally. Among the mineral resources, which are only sketchily explored, are copper, iron, gold, lead, coal and some petroleum. Industrial diamonds are a major export product. Local industries include lumber, soap, textiles, sugar refining, mining and smallscale metal working.

The Angolan population totals approximately five million. Somewhat more than a quarter of a million are of European origin—mostly Portuguese, but with a fair number Dutch and German. Most of the Angolans of African origin belong to five principal tribes (or tribal associations): Bakongo (500,000), who also inhabit the lower Congo region in former Belgian and former French Congo; Kimbundu (1,000,000); Ovimbundu, or Bailundo (1,500,000); Lunda (400,000); Ganguela (400,-000).

2

The Portuguese were the first Europeans to reach Angola: the navigator Diogo Cam (or Cão) touched at the mouth of the Congo in 1482. The first settlers arrived the next year, and there have been Portuguese in Angola ever since—that is, for half a millennium. In the 15th century, the area now called Angola was occupied by Hottentots and Bushmen. These were subsequently conquered and driven out or eaten by the ancestors of the tribes now in Angola, who belong to the Bantu-Negro family. (A few Bushmen survive in the south.) Thus, from a historical standpoint, the Portuguese may more accurately than the Negro tribes be called the "natives" of Angola.

The Catholic Church was established—at first as part of the diocese of Lisbon—in 1491. The ruler of the lower Congo region (Mwani Congo) was baptized shortly thereafter, and in 1534 a cathedral was built at his capital, Bonza Congo, which was re-named São Salvador— the same São Salvador that figures in Mr. Teixeira's narrative. When the cannibals of the interior moved into northern Angola, the Portuguese withdrew further south for a period, and in 1576 founded Luanda, which became the home of more persons of European origin than any other city on the west coast.

However, the Portuguese did not begin extensive development of Angola until the latter part of the 19th century. Before that, their settlements were confined for the most part to the seacoast. In the early centuries, trade was limited to diamonds, gold, small quantities of agricultural produce, and slaves purchased, usually, from the local chiefs for export to the Americas. During the first half of the 19th century, the export of slaves was ended, and in the second half, the institution of slavery was abolished in a series of steps that, for Angola, was completed in 1878. In place of slavery there was instituted a system of "contract labor" through which plantation owners and Portuguese authorities arranged with village chiefs to supply a certain number of workers at such-and-such wages for varying periods of time, often six months. This system lasted until recent years. The Portuguese have defended it as necessary under the social conditions and on the whole humanely organized; but, justifiably or not, it became one of the grievances frequently featured in anti-Portuguese agitation.

As "the scramble for Africa" speeded up, the Portuguese acted to extend their de facto control over the vast territories they had long claimed not only in Angola but in east Africa (Mozambique) and several small enclaves. The Berlin Congress (1884-5) and the arbitration settlement by the King of Italy (1905) confirmed the boundaries of what are still today the Portuguese territories. The quickened rate of development in the present century is suggested by the fact that the white population has increased from 9,000 in 1900 to today's 250,000, and by the increase of four thousand per cent (to about $80 million) in the imports through the port of Luanda.

3

In significant respects the overseas policy of Portugal has differed from that of most other European powers.

1) Portuguese overseas settlement—not merely discovery or purely strategic occupation—began, as we have seen, very long ago, and has been continuous.

2) The Portuguese do not go to an overseas territory merely as "colonials" out to make their fortune or serve their tour of administrative duty, and then return to the home country. Although there are, of course, and have been, such entrepreneurial and administrative colonials, many Portuguese go to the overseas territory as permanent settlers. Angola or Mozambique, or (formerly) Brazil or Goa, not Iberian Portugal, becomes their home; and their "homeland" is the global Portugal that includes both Lisbon and Luanda.

3) British colonialism, in theory, has always conceived the imperial function to involve training the native population to a level at which it can take on self-government and eventually independence. The Catholic Church in European colonies typically sought to enlighten the native population by raising the level of its indigenous culture but at the same time preserving the local cultural elements so far as they could be reconciled with the broad limits of Christian faith. The Portugese approach is different on both counts.

The Portuguese conceive it to be their task to bring Portuguese and Western culture to their overseas subjects; to train them, not to be educated Hottentots or citizens of a severed independent nation, but Portuguese citizens of Portugal. (I refer here to theory, not to practice, which in Angola as in all the European-ruled African territories, has lagged much behind theory. Nevertheless, however laggard, practice has in some measure followed theory.) Following from this premise, for example, all Angolan school lessons and textbooks, even for pupils of African origin, were until recently in the Portuguese language only. At present some African languages are used for texts, but only in bilingual editions, along with Portuguese. Juridically, in consonance with the theory, Angola and Mozambique, like Madeira, are defined not as colonies or dependencies but as provinces of Portugal comparable to the Iberian provinces.

There long existed a juridical rule by which any Angolan of African origin who met certain very small educational and property qualifications could gain all rights of Portuguese citizenship as *assimilado*. (Not all those eligible applied, because citizenship status carried obligations along with rights; but there were about 75,000 *assimilados* in 1960) In September 1961—the intended date was advanced after the shock of the uprising recorded here by Mr. Teixeira—the *assimilado* status was superseded in a law granting full Portuguese citizenship to all Angolans. There is still a small educational and property qualification for voting, but this applies to everyone of whatever race or origin.

4) It is well known that the Portuguese have less color bias than, perhaps, any other people in the world. This is the case in Portugal itself—where one legacy of long Moorish occupation is a wide color spectrum—as in Brazil; and it is the case in Angola. There is no trace of the spirit of apartheid in Angola; no civil rights act and no paratroops are needed to open up public accommoda-

tions to all races. White, black and mulatto are found in the same occupation; three-quarters of the jobs in the administration and bureaucracy are held by non-whites; it is not uncommon, or resented, for a non-white to be bossing a white. Racial inter-marriage is fairly frequent, and brings no difficulty to spouse or children.

It is argued by the critics of Portuguese policy that there is considerable phoneyness in this racial equality, and that in point of fact the whites of Angola are a small privileged class ruling over a large black majority. It is true that whites hold most of the important posts and are on average much better off than the blacks. And it is true that most of the blacks do not have full political rights (e.g., the right to vote in general elections). There may be some concealed color prejudice at work here—it is a rather widespread human trait—but the direct explanation of the better *average* position of the whites is educational and economic, not racial. Moreover, there is an additional equalizing factor in Angola. Most of the Portuguese immigrants in recent decades have been themselves poor peasants. They get modest allotments of land and financial assistance; and they work on their land with their own hands, as they did in Portugal, and as their black neighbors do.

4

On the whole the human conditions in Angola, for the bulk of the population, seem to have been neither the best nor the worst in Africa, but about average. Actually, until lately most of the inhabitants of Angola weren't affected very much one way or another by the presence of white men along the coast. Socially, Angola was something of a backwater, even for Africa, and more sluggish than most of the other colonies. This is expressed in the fact that even at the beginning of 1961, on the date of the terrorist attack, there was in all this vast province a security force of only 8,000 men (2,000 soldiers plus 6,000 local police), of which 5,000 were non-white. This minuscule figure indicates, a) that in Angola as a whole the relations between whites and blacks could not have been very tense, and b) that Portuguese intelligence must have been very poor not to have had some prior inkling of the attack.

During the course of this century, as a larger percentage of the population was drawn from the subsistence villages and jungle into more active economic and social life, political activity began to stir. There were small-scale local uprisings in 1922 and again in 1939. However, until the last decade, most political activity involved not the blacks but the Portuguese inhabitants, who had their grievances against Lisbon's policies, and who were, besides, drawn into the political disputes of metropolitan Portugal. Indeed, Angolan politics have always correlated with and usually subordinated to Portuguese politics; and the Angolan revolutionary movement of the latest period was initiated as an adjunct of the movement aiming to overthrow the Salazar regime in Lisbon.

The first small Angolan political group, the *Liga Afri-*

cana, was founded in 1923. This was followed in 1929 by the *Liga Nacional Africana* and the *Grémio Africano* (which became the *Associação Regional dos Naturais de Angola*—"Regional Association of the Inhabitants of Angola"). The active members of these organizations were mostly Angola-born Portuguese and *assimilados.* Their objectives were limited, and their tactics legal and non-violent; and for more than a decade they were the vehicles for Angola's political life.

In the 1950's the word of revolutionary movements elsewhere began to permeate in Angola, and for the first time independence became the explicit aim of some of the politicalized Angolans. The *Partido da Luta Unida dos Africanos de Angola* ("Party of the United Struggle of the Africans of Angola") was the first revolutionary organization based on the goal of independence and committed to illegal mass tactics. In December 1956 this group formed the *Movimento Popular de Libertação de Angola* (MPLA)—"Popular Movement for the Liberation of Angola."

However, political agitation and organization have never got very far inside Angola. The "mass base" for Angolan nationalist and revolutionary politics has been the several hundred thousand Angolans, mostly Bakongo, who have crossed into the Leopoldville region, looking for jobs or merely wandering about among their tribal brothers. In Leopoldville the aspiring politicians have found recruits and have been able to make contact with sources of money, arms and guidance. As early as 1954 the União das Populações do Norte de Angola ("Union of the People of Northern Angola") was founded in Leopoldville. Its name was changed in 1958 to União das Populações de Angola (UPA)—"Union of the People of Angola"—following the contemporary example of Patrice Lumumba in the Congo in trying to express a nationalist rather than tribal or local conception. This was the organization that mounted the terrorist attack of March 15, 1961.

Also in Leopoldville at this time or somewhat later were the headquarters of two small trade union outfits and a variety of small political groups, most of them— like the ALIAZO (Zombo People's Alliance), the MDIA (Movement for the Defense of Angolan Interest), MLEC (Movement for the Liberation of the Enclave of Cabinde) and the NTO-Abako—connected with a single tribe or personality. Many of these were moderate in policy, and willing to collaborate with the Portuguese, who did in fact educate and find posts for many young people proposed by them. Among this medley, splits, alliances and fronts have succeeded each other with bewildering rapidity.

The MPLA and the UPA proved to be the major revolutionary organizations. Though the former began on a small scale within Angola, it, like the others, has developed primarily outside the country. In March 1959, the Portuguese authorities arrested a number of its local members inside Angola, and thereafter its leadership shifted altogether abroad. The best known MPLA leader, Mário Pinto de Andrade, an *assimilado* of mixed parentage, has, in fact, lived abroad most of his life. During the course of his studies at Lisbon, Paris and Frankfurt Andrade evidently joined both the Portuguese (underground) and the French communist parties. He continued his political training in Warsaw and Moscow, and in 1958 turned up at the Afro-Asian Writers' Conference in Tashkent, Soviet Uzbekistan. He is also known to have spent some time in Peking. In 1959 Andrade set up MPLA headquarters in Conakry, Guinea, then the center of Soviet attempts at African penetration. He entered into close relations with Soviet Ambassador Solod, who arrived later that year to direct West African operations.

The UPA was based abroad from the beginning. Its leader, Holden Roberto (also known as José Gilmore, Roberto Holden, Ruy Ventura, Onofre, etc.), a Negro, was born in 1923 in the same north Angolan town of São Salvador to which several references have already been made. He was educated in a Baptist mission school. He speaks French, English and Portuguese, and is married to Suzana (Susan) Milton, British in origin though born in Angola.

Holden Roberto belongs to a São Salvador tribe of the Bakongo people. His founding of the UPA apparently came about in part as the result of his unsuccessful bid in 1954, backed by the Protestant missionaries against a Catholic claimant, to become Ntotela (king). It was then that he went abroad, where his opinions were progressively radicalized. For a while he settled in Accra, Ghana, where he became acquainted with Nkrumah and, at the first (1958) Pan-African Congress, with many of the revolutionary African leaders as well as some of the

Soviet, Chinese and American agents who swarmed in the conference corridors. He had a job for a while with the Ghanian governmental press services. In this same period Sekou Touré issued him a Guinean passport under the alias of José Gilmore, and, like Andrade, he met Soviet Ambassador Solod in Conakry.

In August, 1959, Holden Roberto visited the United States. While in this country, he was welcomed by several UN delegations, and by the State Department, the Central Intelligence Agency, the AFL-CIO officials concerned with international affairs, and Mrs. Eleanor Roosevelt. These contacts bore fruit; henceforth Roberto and the UPA got both financial and political support from United States sources. He became a well-known figure on the international radical-revolutionary circuit.

Meanwhile Roberto had become an admirer and friend of Patrice Lumumba. After the Congo became independent in July, 1960, Roberto was able to step up UPA preparations in Leopoldville under the benevolent eyes of Lumumba, the UN, the United States, Soviet and Czech embassies, and the Belgian communists whom he had first got to know some years before. Roberto reorganized the UPA along revolutionary and conspiratorial lines, built up its military arm, and prepared the ground for *Der Tag*—the day of March, 1961, that is Mr. Teixeira's subject. Andrade had also returned from Conakry to Leopoldville, and directed his MPLA along a parallel course.

The thirteen hundred mile Angolan-Congolese border —running over mountains and through jungles, swamps and elephant grass—is impossible to police adequately. Roberto was able to send clandestine agents into the north Angolan towns and villages. "Recruits were obtained by the traditional communist tactic of sending leaders into African villages, killing and mutilating a number of men *pour encourager les autres,* and threatening the remainder of the men with like treatment if they did not join the terrorist advance. Wholesale use has been made of the influence of witch doctors, fetishism, and residuary cannibalism."* Roberto succeeded in organizing about 5,000 terrorists in the Congo, armed with machetes and with guns obtained from the old Belgian *Force Publique* members or the new UN army. On the night of 14-15 March, 1961, many of them hopped up with hemp (which grows wild in the area) and other drugs, they struck in the ways described by Bernardo Teixeira.

It seems to have been the strategic conception of the revolutionaries that a ferocious, large-scale terrorist attack would: a) kill enough Portuguese to permit immediate conquest of northern Angola; b) paralyze the Portuguese community as a whole and swamp the meager security force stationed in Angola; c) rouse the entire non-white community, by a combination of terror and promises, to a mass action that would quickly sweep the Portuguese of all Angola into the sea.

Nothing of the sort happened; this strategy proved

---

* "A Catholic View," by Hugh Kay, editor of *Glasgow Observer* and associate editor of *Catholic Herald,* included in the volume, *Angola: Views of a Revolt,* published in 1962 by Oxford Press for the British Institute of Race Relations.

wrong on all counts. The UPA ("Union of the Angolan Peoples"), posing as a national movement for a non-existent nation, was in fact, and remains, basically a tribal organization of the Bakongo. The tribes of central and southern Angola were unmoved by the uprising; and indeed, at its height no more than 25,000 even of the northern Bakongo joined in. The rest stayed either passive or loyal to the Portuguese. The terrorists succeeded in wiping out some of the northern villages and plantations; but—as Mr. Teixeira's account indicates—the settlers managed to rally and hold in a number of the towns. From the small reserve of troops, units were flown to the key points, and within a few days reinforcements began to arrive from Portugal.

The Portuguese, far from being intimidated and paralyzed, were stimulated not merely to resistance but to a more dynamic approach to their African provinces. A long period of bloody conflict followed in the north. The nature of the terrain and the fact that the enemy is based in privileged sanctuary across the border make the problem of pacification enormously difficult. But by the summer of 1964, as Holden Roberto's representative admitted to the Organization for African Unity, order had been generally restored, except for sporadic episodes that under the circumstances could never be altogether eliminated.

Meanwhile the Portuguese, shocked out of their lethargy, and determined that their African territories shall remain part of Western civilization, have stepped up the rate of political and economic development. I have already noted that Lisbon expressed its constitutional perspective by extending Portuguese citizenship to all Angolans in the autumn of 1961. Greatly increased immigration from Portugal has been fostered by grants of land and credits, and by housing and industrial projects. The Portuguese soldiers sent out by the thousands for military duty are encouraged to remain as settlers. The program is restricted, of course, by Portugal's own limited resources. It is interesting to speculate what might have happened if the United States, during these years, had allotted to Angolan development one quarter, say, of the funds that were poured down the Congolese sewer.

5

Although the onslaught of March 1961 failed to bring the revolutionaries the quick and total victory they expected, they have adhered to their goal of "kicking the Portuguese into the sea" (as Roberto has expressed it) and seizing all power in Angola. After a good deal of jockeying back and forth, Holden Roberto's UPA, Mario de Andrade's* MPLA and several minor groups entered into a shaky united front in Leopoldville; and in 1963 declared themselves the Government of Angola. They were duly recognized as such by the Congolese and a number of other African governments. Two large camps near the Angolan border were turned over to them for

* Mario de Andrade himself abandoned the organization at this point and denounced Roberto and his "government in exile."

training their army. Instructors from Algeria, Czechoslovakia, China and elsewhere, together with arms and equipment from a variety of sources, were acquired. A contingent of Roberto's army was a feature of the Congolese independence day parade on July 1, 1964.

Nevertheless, in spite of the support they have received and the favorable geographical position from which they operate, the revolutionaries have done poorly in the military dimension. They can get guerrillas, terrorists, saboteurs and agitators over the border, and these can carry out a certain amount of killings, atrocities, arson and sabotage. But their operations on these fronts have become progressively less effective and less extensive.

Holden Roberto and his advisers do not believe, however, and have probably never believed that armed struggle is their main road to victory. They agree with the judgment of their admirer and volunteer propagandist, Clifford Parsons, former Baptist missionary in Angola, that "militarily, it must appear as though the nationalists have little chance of success."[*] Their primary reliance is on political warfare conduced not in Angola itself but in the world arena: in the many outlets of the world press open to their propaganda, in the Afro-Asian bloc and the United Nations, and in the chancellories of those many nations judging, for one or another reason, that they have something to gain by sailing with the African wind. The campaign of the revolutionaries has therefore been conducted principally in these terms, and on the political

[*] "The Making of a Revolt," by Clifford Parsons; in *Angola, op. cit.*

warfare front has won impressive victories, as the votes in the UN bodies and the anti-Portuguese bias of most of the press demonstrate.

Not the least of the propaganda victories has been the concealment of the events of March 15, 1961. And even today, some readers of this book will wonder: Can these horrors that Bernardo Teixeira recounts really be true? Can they *possibly* be true? Is it conceivable that human beings actually ran other humans through rotary saws and played football with the hacked off limbs of babies? Is not much of this just fiction invented by the Portuguese?

Alas for mankind, not only are these things true, but these things are not the worst of what Holden Roberto's squads did and have done; of some things it is simply not possible to write. A very brief study of the evidence removes any rational doubt. There are the photographs, hundreds of them. There are the carefully checked and collated eye-witness reports. Journalists and diplomatic representatives from many countries, of all political views, went into Angola to find out for themselves, and have verified the atrocities. Though all but two of the authors of the book published by the British Institute of Race Relations, from which I have quoted, are anti-Portuguese, none of them questions the facts.

Nor do Holden Roberto and his associates deny the horrors. At most, they and their defenders counter with the charge that the Portuguese, too, committed atrocities. As to that—which is of course irrelevant to the facts about the March 15 attack—investigation has shown that in the days immediately following March 15, some of the Portuguese settlers whose wives and children had been victims of the terrorists could not be restrained from a vengeance which was, if not in kind, yet very dreadful. In spite of the immense provocation and the inherent difficulty of the security problem, however, the Portuguese soldiers did not carry out, then or later, any counter-atrocities; and the army soon brought the rogue settlers back under control. "I found overwhelming evidence," Mr. Hugh Kay states in the report which I have cited, "to clear the good name of the Portuguese army."

One of the fullest accounts was given in July, 1961, by Pierre de Vos, who had been sent to Africa by the prominent Paris newspaper, *Le Monde*, strongly anti-Portuguese in its editorial position. De Vos quotes at length from Holden Roberto and several of his associates who confirmed the atrocities with perfect frankness; indeed, boasted about them.

" 'The insurgents are accused of the worst of horrors,' " de Vos said to Roberto, " 'and there is proof of tortures perpetrated upon Portuguese men, women and even children, in the areas around São Salvador. Do you deny these massacres?' "

" 'No, all that is true.' "

After then offering the usual justification by long-standing grievances, Roberto concluded: " 'This time the slaves did not cower. They massacred everything (*Ils ont tout massacré*),' "

" 'Women and children included?' " De Vos interjected.

" 'Yes,' Roberto replied. 'Why deny it?' "

De Vos asked one of Roberto's men about the sawmill episode, after recounting that the victims were bound to long boards. " 'Then,' said an Angolan [revolutionary] with a broad smile (*avec un large sourire*), 'we sawed them lengthwise.' "

6

In relation to Angola during these years, as to Africa generally, the policy of the United States has been a compound of ignorance, delusion and short-sighted self-interest of which three, delusion has been the principal ingredient. Our leaders have been maddened by an ideological drug as potent in its effect as the hemp that helped drive Roberto's bestialized savages the morning of March 15, 1961. The abstractions of a debased liberalism, by which our public opinion, like our ship of state, has been guided, warp our vision and confound our action.

It is not necessary to romanticize Portuguese rule in Angola—which has sins enough of commission and omission against its record over the centuries—to realize that the proposed alternative would mean Angola's reduction to a shambles compared to which post-Belgian Congo would seem a Switzerland. Apart from Portuguese sovereignty there is simply no basis—political, social or economic—for the ordered government of Angola. Even at the most elementary level, there is no evidence that the movement of revolt has wide support. The conclusion reached by Mr. Kay after his trip to Angola has not been seriously challenged: "The uprising had little to do with popular movements or spontaneous national combustion." But whatever may be the movement's quantitative extent, it has no serious political content of any kind except among a handful at the top. Questioning of the ordinary followers of Roberto and Andrade invariably reveals that "independence" means to them merely loot— getting houses, autos, women and money, and no work for the rest of their lives.

The outlook for Angola is not hopeless. The southern third of Africa—with vast mineral riches, good harbors, and a sufficiently humane climate and terrain over much of its extent—offers the physical potential for a great new political entity that could develop as an integral part of a reviving Western civilization; and the example of Angola gives hope that all races might there be truly at home. But if the major nations of the West continue to blind themselves to reality and to yield in practice to the demands of black racism and savagery, manipulated coldly by the communist enemy, then Africa's future promises only catastrophe. The true portrait of the African liberation proposed by Roberto, Khrushchev and Mao, and hailed by our own ideologues, has been sketched in this book by Bernardo Teixeira.